Rita Davenport's
SOURDOUGH COOKERY

ANOTHER BEST-SELLING COOKERY VOLUME FROM H.P. BOOKS
This is one of a series of food books which have become America's favorites: *Crockery Cookery* and *Crepe Cookery* by Mable Hoffman, *Sourdough Cookery* by Rita Davenport, *Microwave Cookery* by Richard Deacon, *Italian Cookery* by Pauline Barrese. More of these helpful and modern books are in preparation. H.P. Books give what you expect!

Publisher: Bill Fisher; Editor: Marcia Redding; Managing Editor: Carl Shipman; Art Director: Josh Young; Book Design: Chris Crosson; Typography: Frances Ruiz, Cindy Coatsworth; Photography: George de Gennaro Studios.

ISBN: Soft cover 0-912656-63-8 Hardcover 0-912656-64-6
H.P. Book Number: Softcover 63 Hardcover 64
Library of Congress Catalog Card Number: 77-71168
© 1977, H.P. Books, P.O. Box 5367, Tucson, AZ 85703 602/888-2150
Printed in U.S.A. 3-77

Sourdough Today

For centuries sourdough leavening has been considered mysterious. It is nature's leavening agent.

According to one historical account, sourdough was discovered in the days of the Egyptian Pharoahs about 5,000 years ago. An Egyptian noticed that some flour he had left out in the open had become wet. Bubbles had formed mysteriously in the mixture. When baked into bread, the mixture had a lighter texture and a superior, tantalizing taste.

Today we know that wild airborne yeast fell into the open container of flour and water, causing fermentation. These yeasts are bacteria, similar to bacteria in sour milk or other soured foods, composed of billions of tiny microscopic plants like the organisms found in commercial yeast.

Your sourdough yeast strain is kept alive in a *starter pot* and used again and again as a *starter* for each batch of dough. Each time you use some, replenish as described on page 14 so you don't lose volume and the yeast is nourished to keep it alive and full of bubbles.

During the settlement of the American frontier, miners and trappers carried a pot or crock of sourdough starter with them. The fresh yeast that was available at that time spoiled easily, so sourdough that could be replenished was a valued possession. Some starters became famous for their exceptionally good flavor and were passed down from generation to generation and shared with friends.

The pioneers took extreme care to protect their sourdough starters because they were a dependable and never-ending source of hotcakes, biscuits and bread. Because all of their meals depended on a sourdough starter, these old-timers were appropriately nicknamed "sourdoughs."

Even though it's a heritage from our past, sourdough is as modern as nature itself. Busy, modern people are finding that it doesn't take a lot of time to enjoy the added nutritional value and delicious flavor of sourdough cookery.

Sourdough is appreciated today for more than one good reason. It's natural. Sourdough products are always freshly made and contain no preservatives. It's an inexpensive source of vegetable protein and carbohydrates plus important minerals and B vitamins. And don't forget the flavor!

Sourdough today is used in many more ways than you may imagine. Progressive modern cooks have developed new recipes and approaches to using sourdough in the modern kitchen. Look through this book and you may be surprised!

Sourdough baking will compliment dinner from your electric slow-cooker or oven. The sourdough starter does all the work to leaven and flavor the bread while you are away. At the end of the day, the bread will be ready for baking. Just pop it in the oven and add your personal touch. You'll earn praise and the satisfaction of "doing it yourself." Sourdough is not something you just stir together. It's something you create!

Sourdough cookery is a means of relaxation or maybe your new hobby. There is no limit to the unique and interesting recipes you can create from sourdough—breads, desserts, snacks, pancakes, twists and a multitude of other delights. Experiment, invent and enjoy sourdough.

There may be other helpful benefits from the bacteria in sourdough. Some nutritionists say sourdough aids the digestive bacteria in the intestinal tract. I am not a food chemist or doctor and can't confirm these theories, but I pass them on to you. I personally know of individuals with digestive problems who claim amazing improvement after excluding all but sourdough bread products from their diets. Try it and see.

Whether you seek more natural foods, economy, nutritious and delicious cooking or a creative cooking adventure, sourdough cookery is an answer that fits into the lifestyle of today!

Rita Davenport

SOURDOUGH STARTER

There are two ways to obtain a sourdough starter: By mixing the simple ingredients together yourself or by obtaining a gift of a starter from a friend or family member. The older the starter, the more tangy the flavor. I have used both new and "aged" starters with success.

Because of variations in flour, water composition and local atmospheric conditions, one recipe for starter may be better than another.

The starter is both the *seed yeast* and the nourishment on which the yeast lives. The only requirement for this mixture is that it must be hospitable to the yeast and compatible with bread. Once combined and "started," the sourdough starter contains an everlasting supply of yeast. To better understand its leavening ability, think of this yeast or bacteria as a plant.

During the process of growing, the bacteria gives off carbon-dioxide gas, producing bubbles. It is the bubbles trapped in the dough that cause baked products to rise.

You may be wondering where to obtain atmospheric bacteria to add to your mixture of flour and water. In the wilderness, you merely place the mixture out-of-doors. The organisms are in the air all over the world.

Your only concern may be unfavorable bacteria in the air. If the mixture turns pink or orange, discard immediately and start over. If results from one starter recipe are not excellent, try another.

It is not necessary to place the mixture of flour and water outdoors to attract atmospheric bacteria. You may want to start your mixture indoors. You'll get a good flavor by adding commercially prepared yeast, sugar and salt to a mixture of flour and water. Exact sourdough starter recipes appear later in this book.

Use and replenish your starter once a week and it will live indefinitely, gaining flavor and tang as it grows older. If you are not going to use it for a while, pop it in the freezer for periods up to three months. When you take it out again, let it thaw slowly, stir in a small amount of flour with an equal amount of lukewarm water and let it sit overnight in a warm place. In the morning it should greet you with that familiar, appetizing sourdough aroma.

UTENSILS

An accurate thermometer is a must. Temperature is the single most-important factor in the success of any sourdough recipe. Sourdough needs a temperature close to 85°F (30°C) to work most efficiently while your batter is rising or *proofing.*

Always mix sourdough recipes in glass, stoneware or plastic bowls with plastic or wooden spoons. Remember that any prolonged contact with metal will drastically reduce the purity and change the taste of sourdough.

Use a stoneware or plastic container to store your sourdough starter. Stoneware crocks have traditionally been used as sourdough storage containers. Crocks may be both decorative and practical, but a covered plastic container will work just as well. Make a small hole in the top of the container to allow accumulated gas to escape. Whichever container you chose, it should be large enough to allow for expansion of the starter. Glass or metal containers are not recommended.

Glass or metal loaf pans may be used for baking sourdough breads. The crust thickness and bread texture will vary from pan to pan. Glass pans tend to cause thick crusts while metal pans yield thinner, lighter-colored crusts.

When choosing bowls and pans for sourdough remember that sourdough will often double in volume before baking. It may double again while you bake it.

Most utensils needed for Sourdough Cookery are standard items you probably already have.

The Ingredients

The basic ingredients in many sourdough recipes are: Starter from your starter pot, flour, liquid—either water or milk—plus sugar and salt. The amounts of these ingredients and other items added to the basic mixture will vary from recipe to recipe. However, the basics and the way of mixing them remain the same. I recommend using the best available ingredients. The finished product may be only as good as the worst item used. The ingredients are relatively inexpensive anyway and you save money by doing it yourself, so why not treat yourself to the best?

STARTER

The source of bubbles and flavor in the finished food. Use the amount specified in each recipe. Then replenish the starter as shown on page 14—so you'll have enough next time.

YEAST

Bread leavened only with sourdough starter is sometimes firmer and more chewy than we are accustomed to today. To accommodate modern preference, some recipes in this book call for yeast in addition to starter. This gives light and tender bread with sourdough flavor. You can make bread with sourdough alone by letting it rise twice. This takes longer but the bread has a stronger sourdough flavor.

To get starter, I suggest you follow the recipes and use yeast where called for. When using yeast, follow this procedure:

THE BASICS

Dissolve the yeast in warm water in a warm bowl. Yeast needs a warm, even temperature to work. Too much heat will kill its action and not enough heat will slow the action. Test the water before mixing in the yeast by dropping a small amount on the inside of your wrist. It should feel neither hot nor cold. To warm the bowl, rinse it in hot water and dry thoroughly.

Granular or compressed yeast may be used. Granular yeast is rather dormant. It needs more heat and more moisture to activate it than compressed yeast. If stored in a cool, dry place granular yeast will keep for several months.

Compressed yeast acts quite rapidly when mixed into a dough. It comes in cake form and must be refrigerated. Compressed yeast will keep about two weeks if bought fresh. It may be stored in a freezer and will keep about two months.

FLOUR

Flour should be stirred gently before measuring. This will usually eliminate the need for sifting. Flour is the major ingredient in most sourdough recipes. It is often one of the first ingredients added and more is added at the last in most cases. Flour should be added and mixed in small amounts —about 1/2 cup at a time.

Wheat flour is most often used in bread baking. It contains a substance called *gluten*, which is an elastic protein. When flour is mixed and kneaded with liquid—either water or milk—gluten forms an elastic framework that traps the bubbles of gas produced by leavening. This causes the bread to rise and achieves the desired light texture. Without gluten, a satisfactory yeast-raised or sourdough-leavened bread cannot be produced.

Whole wheat flour also contains bran and wheat germ which furnishes protein, minerals and large amounts of vitamins B and E.

Depending on individual taste and preference, in addition try rye, soy, barley, buckwheat, rice, oat or potato flour. Cornmeal may also be used.

Store flour in a cool, dry place in sealed plastic bags or containers. Flour may be refrigerated or frozen for long-term storage.

LIQUIDS

Liquids suggested for use in sourdough breads are water, water in which potatoes have been cooked, or milk.

Water makes crusty breads with good flavor. Water affects the rising properties of sourdough. The rising time may be longer if very-hard, mineral-laden water is used. Very-soft water may make the dough sticky or soggy.

Potato water may be used as an alternative. It nourishes the leavening bacteria and promotes faster action. Dough made with potato water rises rapidly and often is darker in color.

Bread made with milk has a higher food value. The crust is softer and browner and the bread may stay fresh longer. If fresh milk is used, you may wish to scald it and then cool before using because milk that has not been scalded tends to produce soft dough. The dough-softening action is prevented by heating the milk to approximately 167°F (75°C), a process called *scalding*. Be sure to let the milk cool before using. The harmful ingredient in unheated milk has not been identified, but it is in the whey proteins and its effect is eliminated by heating.

SUGAR

Besides improving flavor, sugar is added to dough to help furnish food for the leavening bacteria. It also aids in the browning process.

White sugar is used most often, but brown sugar, honey or molasses may also be used in some recipes for a slightly different flavor.

SALT

Salt brings out the flavor and aids in controlling the action of the yeast or sourdough starter. It slows the rate of gas formation. Too much salt retards the action of the yeast or starter and a longer fermentation period is required.

FAT

Bread may or may not contain fat—such as margarine, cooking oil, shortening, or butter. Fat makes bread more tender, adds flavor and prevents rapid spoiling. It should be used in small quantities to prevent interference with the formation of gluten in the dough.

EGGS

Some recipes call for eggs. They add food value, enhance flavor and color, and help make the crust tender.

HOW TO CONTROL TEMPERATURE FOR RISING OR PROOFING

When kneading is completed, form the dough into a round ball with a smooth surface. Place the ball in a warm bowl that has been greased with oil or shortening. Turn the dough once to coat the entire surface with oil, to prevent the dough from drying out.

The proper temperature for rising is 80 to 85°F (27 to 30°C). If your kitchen is cool, set the dough on a rack over another bowl containing warm—not boiling—water, which should be changed occasionally as it cools.

Another good location for proofing dough is inside an electric oven. Turn the oven on for a few seconds, just to warm slightly. Turn off, place dough on the inside, near but not touching the oven light. Close door but keep oven light burning for warmth. If the oven doesn't have a light, place a bowl or pan of warm water on the bottom of the oven, under the dough. Change the water as it cools.

If you have a gas range with a pilot light, proofing dough can be near but not touching the pilot light. The top of a refrigerator or hot-water tank may be a good location.

Never expose the sourdough to direct heat. Too much warmth will cause dough to rise too fast which will affect taste and appearance of the finished product.

When beginning a batch of dough, you can use an electric mixer until the dough becomes too stiff and heavy.

As the dough becomes stiffer, finish the job with a wooden spoon, adding flour gradually to get the desired stiffness—usually indicated when the dough pulls away from the sides of the bowl. When this happens, we say the dough "cleans" the bowl.

The Techniques of Sourdough Cookery

To start your starter, select a recipe from this book, mix dry ingredients, then stir in lukewarm water.

When starter is mixed, cover with a towel and set in a warm place (85°F, 30°C) for 2 to 3 days, or until mixture ferments and smells sour but good. Stir occasionally. Use starter according to recipes; replenish as shown on page 14.

Punching down really means just that. Shove your fist into the center of the dough. Then pull the edges of the dough over to the center and turn them down. Don't leave any air pockets.

An easy way to tell if dough has doubled in volume is to press two fingers quickly into the top, about an inch deep.

If the dent stays when you remove your fingers, the dough has risen enough and will be about doubled in volume.

The Techniques of Sourdough Cookery

Dough should be kneaded on a lightly floured surface. Form the dough into a round ball, push it away with the heels of your hands and fold it toward you as you knead.

Turn dough 1/4 turn and repeat the action of pushing the dough away with the heels of your hands and then folding it back toward you. If dough becomes sticky, sprinkle the board with more flour and rub more on your hands.

When the dough has become elastic, with a smooth shiny surface, shape into a ball and allow to proof.

Start shaping a loaf of bread by rolling out the desired amount of dough on a floured board or gently shaping it into a rectangle with your hands.

Form the loaf by rolling up the rectangle of dough. Seal the ends by pressing down with the edges of your hands.

Fold the sealed strips under the loaf and place in baking dish or pan.

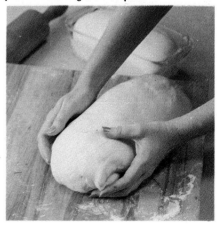

The Techniques of Sourdough Cookery

Newly shaped loaf rises in baking dish until it is ready for the oven.

Test for lightness by pressing lightly with your finger near the edge of the loaf. If the dent stays, it has risen enough.

Oven should be pre-heated to desired temperature. Loaves should be separated in oven to allow heat to reach all sides. Place bread on center shelf of oven. If it browns too rapidly on top, cover with a tent of aluminum foil for the remainder of the baking time.

Rolls can be made in a variety of interesting shapes to bake in muffin tins or on a baking sheet.

HOW TO CONVERT YEAST RECIPES TO SOURDOUGH

Most recipes that call for yeast can be converted to sourdough with minor alterations to the recipe. Whether or not the resulting taste is appealing is a different matter because the taste of sourdough may conflict with another prominent flavor in the recipe. Don't hesitate to experiment. Your successes will outnumber your failures.

The use of yeast makes a lighter product with finer texture. When using sourdough alone as the leavening agent, the rising time will be considerably longer and the product will be firmer and more compact with coarser texture.

For One Large Loaf of Bread or Equivalent:
Omit the recommended amount of yeast.

Omit 1-3/4 cup of liquid from the original recipe. You can omit eggs and consider each large egg equivalent to 1/4 cup of liquid.

Add 2 cups of sourdough starter. When you add starter, you put back the leavening agent, plus some liquid, plus some flour, all contained in the starter.

Reduce the amount of dry flour in the recipe by one cup because that's the amount of flour in 2 cups of sourdough starter.

Do not change the amount of cooking oil.

For Two Large Loaves of Bread or Equivalent:
The basic idea is the same but quantities double. Omit the recommended amount of yeast.

Omit 3-1/2 cups of liquids, counting large eggs as 1/4 cup each.

Add 4 cups of starter.

Reduce the amount of dry flour by 2 cups.

When Liquid in the Recipe Contributes to Flavor:
In recipes where the flavor is derived from a liquid ingredient such as a puree or eggs, it may not be possible to leave out the amount of liquid recommended above without omitting some of the fluid that gives the desired flavor.

In that case, just add one cup of sourdough starter to the original recipe. This will give a good sourdough flavor. If the mixture appears too moist, add and mix in a half-cup of flour.

That allows you to leave in the flavoring liquids of the original recipe. It may not use as much starter as other recipes. Just give it more time to proof and the sourdough will work fine.

STORING SOURDOUGH BAKED GOODS

Because of the healthy, active bacteria in sourdough, and the absence of chemical preservatives, here are some special storing hints to keep your baked goods at their best.

Sourdough products will keep for a couple of days in bread boxes or other containers which retard drying. Individual loaves may be wrapped in wax paper or plastic wrap.

Temperature is a big factor in storing sourdough products. To keep baked items for several days, wrap and store in the refrigerator.

Sourdough baked goods freeze well and can be kept up to 3 months this way. When ready to use, just thaw and serve.

CAUSES OF INFERIOR BREAD

PROBLEM	CAUSE
Poor texture, color, volume or heaviness	Inferior, inexpensive flour
Coarse texture or dry crumb	Too much flour
Bread won't rise	Over-kneading or inactive yeast
Streaked loaf	Under-kneading, poor mixing, or drying top of dough before shaping
Uneven shape	Too much dough for pan, improper molding or shaping
Porous bread with pale crumbling crust	Over-rising
Flat loaf that browns too quickly	Under-rising
Thick crust	Baking too slowly
Crackled crust	Too rapid cooling in draft
Tough Crust	Inferior flour, too much salt, too much handling
Pale Crust	Too little sugar, too much salt, too slow an oven, or drying of dough during rising
Undesirable Taste	Rising too long, inferior yeast or flour, too high temperature while rising or too slow or incomplete baking
Cracks and bulging crust	Uneven heat in baking or too stiff dough

Starters

To show how modern and versatile sourdough has become, here are ten different recipes for starters. The old-timer's idea was to get one good starter, guard it carefully, nourish it to keep it alive and use it indefinitely.

That's still a good idea, but starters are easy to create in a modern kitchen, so you don't have to limit yourself to just one. Naturally you will use the Basic Sourdough Starter because it really is basic and the most useful of all. After you get a pot of basic starter bubbling, then try some of the others I have included here.

Starter is the beginning of all sourdough foods. It is important to understand what a sourdough starter is, how it works and how it is cared for before using the recipes in this book. You will be surprised at how easy it really is. You'll create and maintain a bubbling aromatic pot of sourdough starter that will become a trusted friend and helper in your kitchen.

To survive in your starter, the yeast needs a warm, but not hot environment, moisture and a continuous food source in the form of a starchy product. Wheat, rye, cornmeal, potatoes and rice can all be used to nourish the yeast in your starter.

After measuring out the correct amount of sourdough starter for your recipe, replenish the starter by adding equal portions of flour and water or some bubbly batter mixture before you add other ingredients. Allow to sit overnight in a warm place covered with a cloth or plastic wrap. Return to the refrigerator for storing. Never add anything to your starter except flour and water and a sprinkle of dry yeast when needed to liven up the mixture.

Some people are starting their sourdough starter in home-type cheese and yogurt makers with good results. After fermentation is completed, store in the refrigerator in a covered container.

You'll soon be mixing and matching different starters with different types of food—another way of expressing your creativity in the kitchen.

Starter shown at top is freshly mixed. As it ferments, bubbles form as shown in container at right. When fully developed, it looks like starter shown in foreground. Yellow liquid on top is alcohol which Alaskan Indians called *hooch.* When it forms, just stir it back into the mixture.

Basic Sourdough Starter

I used this starter for most of the recipes in this cookbook.

2 cups all-purpose flour
1 teaspoon salt
3 tablespoons sugar

1 tablespoon dry yeast
2 cups lukewarm water

With a wooden spoon stir dry ingredients together in a large mixing bowl and gradually add luke-warm water. Stir until mixture resembles a smooth paste. Cover with a towel or cheesecloth and set in a warm place—85°F (30°C)—to sour. Stir mixture several times a day. In 2 or 3 days sourdough will be ready. Store in a heavy plastic container, with a hole punched in lid to allow gases to escape.

To make a batter for a favorite sourdough recipe, take out 1 cup sourdough starter and combine with 1 cup all-purpose flour and 1 cup lukewarm water. Mix well with a wooden spoon. Don't worry about lumps in mixture, fermentation will dissolve them within a few hours. Cover with a towel or plastic wrap and set in a warm location several hours or overnight. *Before adding additional ingredients to recipe,* return at least 1/2 cup of mixture to sourdough container stored in refrigerator to replenish starter.

If starter is not replenished in this manner at least once a week, add 1/2 cup each of lukewarm water and all-purpose flour to container of sourdough. Mix together; leave out of refrigerator over-night, covered with a towel or plastic wrap. Next morning stir down mixture, cover with lid and return to refrigerator until needed.

Occasionally pour all of sourdough starter out into a mixing bowl. Wash container to remove flour buildup. To replenish, add equal portions of flour and water, cover, let stand in a warm—85°F (30°C)—location overnight.

If starter does not seem as bubbly after continued use, sprinkle with small amount of dry yeast and mix well. This is also recommended if thawed frozen starter does not resume its former bubbly appearance. If clear liquid forms on top of mixture, simply stir down and continue to use as needed.

HOW TO REPLENISH YOUR STARTER
The first step in preparation of many recipes in this book is to measure out the required amount of starter, taking it from your starter pot. Add equal portions of flour and lukewarm water, following the recipe for the item you are making.

Cover with a towel or plastic wrap and set in a warm place (80 to 85°F) over-night.

Next morning, before adding any other ingredients to mixture, return at least 1/2 cup of the mixture to your starter pot. Store starter pot in refrigerator. Re-plenish once a week.

Quick, Overnight Sourdough Starter

This gives a mild sourdough flavor in a hurry.

1 pkg. plus 1 tablespoon dry yeast   4 cups all-purpose flour
4 cups lukewarm water

Dissolve yeast in a small amount of lukewarm water. Stir flour into remaining water and add yeast mixture. Mix well and cover. Let mixture stand in a draft free area that is near 85°F (30°C) for at least 6 hours or overnight. Starter is now ready to be mixed with other ingredients for your favorite sourdough recipe.

Whole Wheat Sourdough Starter

The full, satisfying flavor of whole wheat combined with the tang of sourdough.

1/2 teaspoon dry yeast   3/4 cup whole wheat flour
3/4 cup warm water (110°F, 43°C)

Dissolve yeast in warm water. Stir in flour and mix well. Store in a clean, covered plastic container large enough to allow for expansion. Place in a warm area for 18 to 20 hours. Stir occasionally. At this point starter may be stored in refrigerator and will be referred to as primary batter or starter.

Keep whole wheat starters separate from other starters to provide desired flavor and texture for different recipes. Keep starter active by adding equal portions of whole wheat flour and water at least once a week if starter is not replenished with normal use.

Potato Water Sourdough Starter

Use the potatoes for dinner, save the water for this starter.

3 medium potatoes, peeled and cubed   1 tablespoon salt
1 qt. water   1 pkg. dry yeast
1-3/4 cups all-purpose flour   2-1/2 cups potato water
1 tablespoon sugar

Cook approximately 3 medium potatoes in water until tender. Drain, reserving liquid. Use potatoes in a favorite recipe. In a medium sized mixing bowl combine flour, sugar, salt and dry yeast. Mix well. Stir in reserved potato water. Cover with a towel or cheesecloth and place in a warm place—85°F (30°C)—for 1 to 2 days or until mixture becomes bubbly. Stir down several times a day. Store until needed in refrigerator in a clean plastic container with tight fitting lid. The lid must have a small hole punched in it to allow gases to escape. To replenish add equal amounts of all-purpose flour and lukewarm water at least once a week.

Peasant Bread Starter

Use this with whole-wheat flour recipes.

1 pkg. dry yeast

1-1/2 cups warm water (110°F, 43°C))

1 tablespoon non-fat powdered milk

1 cup whole wheat flour

In a 2-quart glass mixing bowl dissolve yeast in water. Add milk and whole wheat flour. Mix thoroughly. Cover with a clean towel, place in a warm–85°F (30°C)–location for 24 hours. Stir down mixture often. Mixture should be thick and bubbly. Starter is now ready to be used or stored in the refrigerator in a covered plastic container with a vent hole until needed as part of the recipe for whole-wheat breads. Replenish with equal amounts of warm water and whole wheat flour at least once a week. If a clear liquid collects on top of mixture, stir down and use as directed. This starter is recommended for use in Peasant Bread or other whole wheat recipes. Be careful not to store for fermenting in an area that is over 90°F (32°C). If starter becomes inactive, sprinkle with a small amount of yeast and mix well. Lumps in mixture will disappear with fermentation.

Sour Rye Starter

This is the one to use with rye-flour recipes for that true rye flavor.

2 cups rye flour

1-1/2 cups warm water (105° to 110°F)

1 pkg. dry yeast

1 slice onion

Mix the flour, water, yeast and onion together in a quart container. Cover with a clean cloth and place in a warm location–85°F (30°C)–for 3 or 4 days or until it is well fermented as indicated by a frothy appearance and a pleasant sour aroma. Remove the onion. Starter is now ready to be used or stored in the refrigerator in a covered plastic container until needed in sourdough rye breads. Be sure a small hole is punched in cover of container to allow gases to escape. Also fermentation should not occur in a location above 90°F (32°C) for best results. To keep starter active, feed with equal portions of warm water and rye flour. A small amount of yeast sprinkled over top of mixture may be needed if starter doesn't appear active and bubbly.

Sourdough Yogurt Starter

Yogurt fans will be delighted with this one.

1 cup milk   1 cup all-purpose flour
2 tablespoons yogurt, low-fat or plain unflavored

Heat milk until it reaches 100°F (38°C) on a thermometer. Remove from heat and stir in yogurt. Pour mixture into a clean plastic container, cover tightly and let stand in a warm place for 18 to 24 hours. Be sure to punch a small hole in container lid to allow gases to escape. Mixture should resemble the consistency of yogurt. A curd should form and the mixture should not flow readily when the container is slightly tilted. If clear liquid rises to the top of mixture, simply stir it back in. If liquid or starter turns pink, discard mixture and start again. After curd has formed, gradually stir 1 cup flour into the starter until smoothly blended. Cover tightly and let stand in a warm place—85°F (30°C)—until mixture is full of bubbles and has a good sour smell, approximately 2 to 5 days. If clear liquid forms on top of mixture, stir it back into starter. Each time you use part of your starter replenish it with equal amounts of warm milk—100°F (38°C)—and flour. Cover and let stand in a warm place several hours or overnight until it is full of bubbles. Cover and store in refrigerator until needed. Starter should always be at room temperature before using. Low-fat or skim milk may be used in place of whole milk. Always be consistent in type of milk used.

Honey Starter

For individuals who exclude sugar from their diets, this is a very popular starter.

1 pkg. dry yeast   2 tablespoons honey
2-1/2 cups warm water (110°F, 43°C)   2-1/2 cups all-purpose flour

Combine the yeast, water, honey and flour in a 2-quart glass mixing bowl. Cover with cheesecloth, place in a warm area—85°F (30°C)—to ferment. In 2 or 3 days sourdough will be ready for use. Use, or store in a clean plastic container with a fitted cover in refrigerator until needed. Be sure a hole is punched in container lid to allow gases to escape. If a clear liquid collects on top of mixture, stir down when ready to use. Replenish at least once a week with equal portions of warm water and all-purpose flour.

Raw Potato Starter

Pioneers used this starter.

1 cup warm water (110°F, 43°C)
1-1/4 cups all-purpose flour
1 teaspoon salt

1-1/2 teaspoons sugar
1 medium potato, peeled and grated

Mix together the water, flour, salt and sugar in a 1-quart glass mixing bowl. Add grated potato and mix well. Cover container tightly with plastic wrap to prevent moisture from evaporating and allow it to sit in a warm place—85°F (30°C)—for 24 hours. Stir several times during the 24-hour period. Within 2 or 3 days mixture will become fermented, giving a foamy appearance. Stir down at least once each day. Pour the fermented starter into a clean plastic 1-quart container. Cover with a fitted lid that has a small hole punched to allow gases to escape. After being refrigerated for 3 to 4 days, mixture will be ripened sufficiently to use. A clear liquid will collect on top. Simply stir into mixture and use starter when needed. Replenish the starter with equal portions of warm water and flour. Allow to sit at room temperature 10 to 12 hours then return to refrigerator until needed.

Mashed Potato Sourdough Starter

Don't throw out those cold mashed potatoes—make a starter.

1 cup cooked mashed potatoes
1/4 cup sugar

2 teaspoons salt
1 cup warm water (110°F, 43°C)

Put 1 cup of cooked mashed potato in a clean quart container. Add sugar, salt and warm water. Mix well. Cover with a clean towel and place in a warm location for two days or until mixture ferments, bubbles up and smells pleasantly sour. Use at this time or store in the refrigerator in a clean plastic container. Cover of container should have a small hole punched to allow gases to escape. Sourdough breads made from this starter will not taste any different than any other starter or have any of the flavor of potatoes. Replenish with equal portions of flour and warm water added to starter. Allow to ferment at room temperature for 8 to 10 hours and then return, covered to refrigerator. If starter is not used and replenished once a week, stir down after 3 or 4 weeks, discard half of it and replenish the balance with same recipe first used. A sprinkle of dry yeast may be needed if starter doesn't appear bubbly and fermented after being in use for a period of time. If a clear liquid forms on top of mixture, simply stir down and continue to use as needed.

Sourdough Breads

You'll probably feel you've mastered breadbaking and developed a complete understanding of sourdough cookery when you slice and serve your very first successful loaf of sourdough bread. You're right! All that's left is to explore the wonderful variety of sourdough breads you can make.

There are so many delicious breads in this section it's hard to choose a favorite. Sourdough Cheese Swirl is delicious and showy; Sourdough Spinach Bread is almost a meal by itself; Sourdough Taco Twist is for anyone who enjoys southwestern flavors.

The most important ingredient in breadmaking is patience. The results will be well worth waiting for, but you must remember that you cannot rush the fermentation or proofing process that prepares the dough for baking. A temperature that's too high will kill the bacteria; too cold will discourage growth.

Besides patience and temperature control there is something else that can be a tricky part of breadmaking—using the right amount of flour. So many factors affect the correct proportion: The consistency of your sourdough starter, the humidity on the day you bake, and even the milling or type of flour used and its compactness. For this reason I recommend that you never add all the flour called for in a recipe, all at once. Add and mix one-half to one cup at a time, working the last 1 or 2 cups in during kneading. This will help keep your dough from being too dry. A good way to determine if dough has been kneaded long enough to develop the gluten is to pinch the dough and at the same time squeeze your ear lobe. They will feel about the same when the dough is ready for shaping.

Experience will quickly teach you how to tell when a loaf of bread is done. Look for an even, deep golden-brown color. Thump the top of the loaf, near the center, and it should have a hollow sound that tells you it is firm inside. If you press the top gently, it doesn't give.

Sourdough Bread

Ever get hungry for just plain, old-fashioned sourdough bread? Bake this and rejoice.

1 cup sourdough starter
2 cups lukewarm water
2-1/2 cups all-purpose flour
1 cup milk
3 tablespoons butter or margarine, softened
3 tablespoons sugar

2 teaspoons salt
1 pkg. dry yeast
1/4 cup warm water (110°F, 43°C)
6-1/2 cups all-purpose flour
1 teaspoon baking soda
Cooking oil

Measure starter into large bowl. Add 2 cups lukewarm water and 2-1/2 cups flour. Mix well. Let stand, covered, in warm place overnight. The next morning heat milk; then stir in butter or margarine, 2 tablespoons sugar and 1 teaspoon salt. Cool to lukewarm. Sprinkle yeast over 1/4 cup warm water. Let stand 5 minutes. Stir yeast into cooled milk mixture. Add to starter mixture. Beat until well mixed. Beat in 2 cups flour until batter is smooth. Mix baking soda with remaining tablespoon of sugar and teaspoon of salt. Sift evenly over dough and stir gently to mix well. Cover with a cloth. Set in warm place free from drafts and let rise 30 to 40 minutes or until almost doubled in size. Mix dough and gradually beat in rest of the flour until dough is stiff enough to clean sides of bowl. Turn out onto floured surface and knead about 5 minutes or until smooth and elastic, adding more flour if necessary. Divide dough in half. Let rest, covered, for 10 minutes. Grease 2 loaf pans. Shape loaves and place in pans. Brush tops lightly with cooking oil. Let rise about 1 hour until dough has risen to top of pans. Bake at 375°F (191°C) for 50 minutes or until done. Makes 2 loaves.

Sourdough French Bread

Cornmeal gives this bread a hint of English muffins.

1 pkg. dry yeast
1-1/2 cups warm water (110°F, 43°C)
5 to 5-1/2 cups all-purpose flour
1 cup sourdough starter
3 tablespoons sugar

2 tablespoons butter, melted
2 teaspoons salt
1/2 teaspoon baking soda
1 teaspoon yellow cornmeal

In large mixing bowl, soften yeast in water. Blend in 2 cups of the flour, sourdough starter, sugar, butter and salt. Combine 1 cup of the flour and baking soda. Stir into flour-yeast mixture. Add enough remaining flour to make a moderately stiff dough. Turn out onto floured surface and knead 5 to 8 minutes or until smooth. Place in greased bowl, turning once. Cover with a cloth. Set in warm place free from drafts and let rise for 1 to 1-1/2 hours or until doubled in size. Punch down dough and divide in half. Cover and let rest 10 minutes. Shape in 2 oblong or round loaves. Place on greased baking sheet sprinkled with cornmeal. Cover. Let rise in warm place about 1 hour or until almost doubled in size. Brush with water and make diagonal slashes across tops with a sharp knife or single-edge razor blade. Bake at 375°F (191°C) for 30 to 35 minutes. Remove from sheet and cool. Makes 2 loaves.

San Francisco Style Sourdough French Bread

Serve a touch of San Francisco to your guests.

1-1/2 cups warm water (110°F, 43°C)
1 tablespoon or 1 pkg. dry yeast
1 cup sourdough starter
3 cups all-purpose flour

2 teaspoons sugar
2 teaspoons salt
1 teaspoon baking soda
2 cups additional all-purpose flour

In a large mixing bowl dissolve yeast in warm water. Mix with starter. Add 3 cups flour, sugar and salt. Stir vigorously 2 or 3 minutes. Cover with a cloth. Set in warm place and let rise 1-1/2 to 2 hours or until doubled in size. Mix baking soda with 1 cup of remaining flour and stir in. The dough should be stiff. Turn out onto a floured surface and begin kneading. Add the remaining 1 cup of flour or more if needed to control stickiness. Knead until satiny, between 5 and 10 minutes. Shape into 2 oblong loaves or 1 large round loaf. Place on lightly greased cookie sheet. Cover with a cloth. Set in warm place free from drafts and let rise 1 to 2 hours or until nearly doubled in size. Before baking, brush outside with water and make diagonal slashes across the top with a sharp single-edge razor blade. Put a shallow pan of hot water in the bottom of the oven. Bake at 400°F (205°C) for 45 minutes or until the crust is a medium dark brown. Makes 2 loaves.

Note:
You may wish to brush top of loaves before baking with 1 teaspoon cornstarch mixed with 1/2 cup water or an egg yolk or whole egg beaten with 1 to 2 tablespoons water. If using cornstarch, heat to boiling while stirring. Cool slightly.

Quick Sourdough Bread

An easy bread for the beginner.

2 cups sourdough starter
1 teaspoon dry yeast
3 tablespoons warm water (110°F, 43°C)
3 tablespoons sugar

1-1/2 teaspoons salt
3 tablespoons powdered milk
2 tablespoons melted shortening or cooking oil
3 to 4 cups all-purpose flour

Measure out sourdough starter. In a small separate bowl dissolve yeast in warm water. Add to sourdough starter along with sugar, salt, powdered milk and shortening or cooking oil. Mix well. Slowly add the flour until the dough pulls away from side of the bowl. Turn out onto a floured surface and knead until smooth and elastic, adding more flour if necessary. Shape the dough and place in a well greased loaf pan. Cover with a cloth. Set in a warm place free from drafts and let rise until doubled in size. Bake at 350°F (177°C) for 50 minutes or until done. Makes 1 loaf.

Sourdough Cheese Swirl

Delicious served hot or cold.

2 cups sourdough starter
1 teaspoon dry yeast
3 tablespoons warm water (110°F, 43°C)
3 tablespoons sugar
1 teaspoon salt
2 tablespoons cooking oil or melted shortening

3 tablespoons powdered milk
3-1/2 to 4 cups all-purpose flour
1 cup shredded Cheddar cheese
1 to 2 tablespoons dry onion-soup mix or
    onion-dip mix
Melted butter

Measure sourdough starter into a large mixing bowl. Dissolve yeast in warm water. Add to sourdough starter along with sugar, salt, oil or shortening and powdered milk. Gradually add flour until dough pulls away from the side of the bowl. Turn out onto a floured surface and knead until elastic and smooth, 5 to 7 minutes. Roll out dough to an 8" x 12" rectangle. Sprinkle with cheese and onion-soup mix or dip mix. Roll up jelly-roll style, beginning with narrow side. Place in a greased loaf pan. Cover with a cloth and place in a warm place free from drafts and let rise until doubled in size. Bake at 350°F (177°C) for 50 minutes or until done. Brush top with melted butter. Delicious served hot or cold. Makes 1 cheese swirl loaf.

Note:
4 to 5 slices of fried crumbled bacon is delicious added along with cheese and onion-soup mix or dip mix.

Cottage Cheese Sourdough Bread

A delightful blend of cheeses.

2 tablespoons or 2 pkgs. dry yeast
2 cups lukewarm water
1 cup sourdough starter
2 cups creamed cottage cheese
2 cups grated sharp or longhorn cheese
1/2 teaspoon baking powder

2 tablespoons dill seed
2 tablespoons cooking oil or melted shortening
2 tablespoons sugar
2 tablespoons salt
6-1/2 to 7-1/2 cups all-purpose flour

Dissolve yeast in lukewarm water. Measure sourdough starter into a large mixing bowl. Add cheeses, baking powder, dill seed, oil or margarine, sugar and salt to sourdough starter. Add dissolved yeast. Gradually beat in flour 1/2 cup at a time, stirring well after each addition. Reserve 1/2 cup flour to work into dough during kneading. Dough should be fairly stiff. Turn out onto lightly floured surface and knead for 5 to 10 minutes, adding reserved flour if necessary. Put in a greased bowl, turning once. Cover with a cloth. Set in warm place free from drafts and let rise for 2 hours or until doubled in size. Punch dough down. Shape into 2 loaves and cover with a cloth. Set in warm place free from drafts and let rise for 2 hours or until doubled in size. Bake in a well greased loaf pan at 375°F (191°C) for 40 minutes. Makes 2 loaves.

Sourdough Wheat Bread

Nutty, wholesome flavor.

1 pkg. dry yeast
1-1/2 cups warm water (110°F, 43°C)
3 cups whole wheat flour
1 cup sourdough starter
1/4 cup dark molasses

3 tablespoons butter, softened
2 teaspoons salt
2-1/2 to 3 cups unbleached white flour or
   all-purpose flour
1/2 teaspoon baking soda

In large mixing bowl soften yeast in warm water. Blend in whole wheat flour, sourdough starter, molasses, butter and salt. Combine 1 cup of unbleached white or all-purpose flour and baking soda. Stir into flour-yeast mixture. Add enough remaining flour to make a moderately stiff dough. Turn out onto floured surface and knead 5 to 8 minutes or until smooth. Shape into a ball. Place in a greased bowl, turning once. Cover with a cloth. Set in warm place free from drafts and let rise 1-1/2 to 2 hours or until doubled in size. Punch down and divide in half. Cover. Let rest 10 minutes. Shape in 2 loaves and place in two greased loaf pans. Cover. Let rise about 1 hour or until doubled in size. Bake at 375°F (191°C) for 35 to 40 minutes. Remove from pans. Cool. Makes 2 loaves.

Sourdough Whole Wheat French Bread

A nutritious version of an old-time favorite.

1 pkg. dry yeast
1-1/2 cups warm water (110°F, 43°C)
1-1/2 cups sourdough starter
4-1/2 cups whole wheat flour

1 tablespoon sugar
1-1/2 teaspoons salt
1/2 teaspoon baking soda
1-1/2 to 2 cups additional flour

In large mixing bowl dissolve yeast in warm water. Let stand 10 minutes. Mix in sourdough starter; blend well. Stir in 4-1/2 cups whole wheat flour, sugar and salt. Stir vigorously for 3 to 4 minutes. Cover with a cloth. Set in warm place free from drafts and let rise about 2 hours or until doubled in size. Combine baking soda and 1 cup whole wheat flour. Stir into batter. Turn out onto well floured surface and knead 8 to 10 minutes, adding more whole wheat flour if necessary. Shape into 2 oblong loaves. Place on greased cookie sheet. Cover with a cloth. Let rise in a warm place free from drafts for 1 to 2 hours or until doubled in size. Brush loaves with water. Make 3 diagonal slashes on top of each loaf with a sharp knife. Put a shallow pan of hot water on the bottom of the oven. Bake at 400°F (205°C) for 45 to 50 minutes or until golden brown. Makes 2 loaves.

Sourdough Whole Wheat Pan Bread

When the top crust browns just enough, cover with a tent of aluminum foil.

2/3 cup nonfat dry powdered milk
2 cups lukewarm water
1 pkg. dry yeast
3 cups whole wheat flour
4-1/2 cups all-purpose flour

3/4 cup sourdough starter
1/4 cup molasses
1 tablespoon salt
3 tablespoons soft margarine
1 teaspoon baking soda

Combine powdered milk, lukewarm water and yeast. Add whole wheat flour and 1 cup all-purpose flour and sourdough starter. Mix well. Cover and place in a warm area. Allow to proof for 1 to 2 hours. Add the molasses, salt, margarine and baking soda. Gradually mix in enough of the remaining flour to form a stiff dough. Turn out onto floured surface and knead for 10 minutes or until smooth and elastic. Put in greased bowl, turning once. Cover with a cloth. Set in warm place free from drafts and let rise about 1 to 2 hours or until doubled in size. Punch down dough and divide in half. Shape into loaves and put into well greased loaf pans. Cover with cloth. Set in warm place free from drafts and let rise about 2 hours or until doubled in size. Bake at 375°F (191°C) for 45 minutes. Makes 2 loaves.

Sourdough Applesauce-Wheat Bread

Brown sugar and applesauce combine flavors to create this delicious whole wheat bread.

1 pkg. dry yeast or 1 cake compressed yeast
1/4 cup warm water (110°F, 43°C)
1 cup sourdough starter
1/4 cup cooking oil
1/2 cup brown sugar, firmly packed
1-1/2 cups applesauce

1 tablespoon salt
1 cup hot water
3 cups whole wheat flour
1/4 teaspoon baking soda
3 to 4 cups all-purpose flour
Melted butter

Mix together yeast and warm water. Stir until dissolved and set aside. In a large mixing bowl combine sourdough starter with oil, brown sugar, applesauce, salt, hot water, whole wheat flour and baking soda. Mix well. Let rest for 10 minutes. Blend in softened yeast mixture. Gradually add flour as needed to make a moderately stiff dough. Turn out onto floured surface and knead 10 minutes, adding more flour if necessary. Place in a greased bowl, turning once. Cover with a cloth. Set in warm place free from drafts and let rise for 1 to 2 hours or until doubled in size. Punch down dough. Shape in 2 loaves. Place in greased loaf pans. Cover with a cloth and let rise in a warm place free from drafts until almost doubled in size. Bake at 350°F (177°C) for 35 to 45 minutes. Brush with melted butter. Makes 2 loaves.

Sourdough Oatmeal Bread

For a light texture allow plenty of time to rise before baking.

1-1/2 cups sourdough starter
1 cup lukewarm milk
1/4 cup brown sugar, firmly packed
1/2 cup molasses
2 teaspoons salt

3 tablespoons melted shortening or cooking oil
2 cups rolled oats
2 to 2-1/2 cups all-purpose flour
Melted butter

Measure sourdough starter into a large bowl. Add lukewarm milk, brown sugar, molasses, salt and melted shortening. Add rolled oats, 1/2 cup at a time, mixing well after each addition. Stir in 1-1/4 cups flour and turn out onto a floured surface. Knead until smooth and elastic, adding more flour if necessary. Place in a greased bowl, turning once. Cover. Set bowl in a warm place free from drafts and let rise for 2 hours or until doubled in size. Punch down dough. Turn out onto a surface and separate into 2 pieces. Shape into loaves and place in well greased loaf pans. Brush tops with melted butter and cover with a cloth. Set pans in a warm place free from drafts and let rise for 1-1/2 hours. Bread should rise until it reaches top of pans. Bake at 400°F (205°C) for 35 to 40 minutes. Makes 2 loaves.

Sourdough Cheese Bread

Try this with crumbled bacon bits added to the cheese.

1-1/2 cups sourdough starter
1-1/4 cups lukewarm milk
1/2 cup sugar
2 teaspoons salt
1 egg, slightly beaten

3 tablespoons melted butter or margarine
2 cups grated sharp Cheddar cheese
1/4 teaspoon baking soda
3 to 4 cups all-purpose flour
Melted butter

To sourdough starter add lukewarm milk, sugar and salt. Beat well. Add slightly beaten egg, melted butter or margarine and grated cheese. Add baking soda to flour. Stir in flour 1 cup at a time, stirring after each addition. Reserve at least 1/2 cup of flour to add during kneading process. Turn out onto floured surface and knead until it is smooth and elastic. Shape into loaves and place in greased loaf pans. Brush with melted butter. Cover with a cloth. Set in warm place free from drafts and let rise for about 2 hours or until doubled in size. Bake at 375°F (191°C) for 30 minutes. If bread begins to brown too soon, cover with a tent of aluminum foil. Makes 2 loaves.

Sourdough Herb Twist

A blend of Italian seasoning and Cheddar cheese for a special taste delight.

1 cup sourdough starter	1 egg
1/2 cup onion salad dressing	1-1/2 teaspoons Italian seasoning
1 pkg. dry yeast	1 cup shredded Cheddar cheese
1/3 cup warm water (110°F, 43°C)	1 teaspoon salt
1 tablespoon sugar	3 to 4 cups all-purpose flour

Measure out sourdough starter in a large mixing bowl. Add salad dressing. Mix well. Dissolve yeast in warm water. Add to sourdough mixture along with sugar, egg, Italian seasoning, cheese and salt. Mix well by hand. Add enough flour until the dough cleans the side of the bowl. Turn out onto floured surface; knead until smooth and elastic, about 2 minutes. Place in greased bowl, turning once. Cover with a cloth. Set in warm place free from drafts and let rise 45 to 60 minutes or until doubled in size. Grease a 9" x 5" loaf pan. Divide dough into 2 parts. Shape each into a roll 10 inches long. Twist rolls together and place in greased loaf pan. Cover with a cloth. Let rise again in a warm place free from drafts, 50 to 60 minutes or until doubled in size. Bake at 375°F (191°C) for 30 to 40 minutes or until golden brown. Remove from pan immediately. Makes 1 twist.

Divide the dough into 2 parts. Shape each into a roll 10-inches long.

Twist the 2 rolls together and place in greased loaf pan.

Sourdough Sally Lunn

Delicious with butter and marmalade.

1/2 cup butter
1/3 cup sugar
1-1/2 cups sourdough starter
1 cup lukewarm milk

3 eggs, beaten
1 teaspoon salt
4 to 4-1/2 cups all-purpose flour

Cream together butter and sugar. Add sourdough starter. Mix well. Alternately add milk and beaten eggs. Mix together salt and flour. Add to sourdough mixture and beat until smooth. Cover with a cloth. Set in warm place free from drafts and let rise until doubled in size. Stir down and pour into a greased cake pan or loaf pan. Let rise again until doubled in size. Bake at 350°F (177°C) for 45 minutes or until golden brown and springy. Serve hot or cold. Cut in wedges or slice. Makes 1 cake or loaf.

Sourdough Spinach Bread

The filling is superb—and good for you!

Bread:
1-1/2 cups lukewarm water
2 cups all-purpose flour
1-1/2 cups sourdough starter
1 cup milk
3 tablespoons butter or margarine
3 tablespoons sugar

2 teaspoons salt
1 pkg. dry yeast
1/4 cup warm water (110°F, 43°C)
6 to 7 cups all-purpose flour
Egg yolk

Filling:
3 pkgs. frozen spinach, cooked and drained
2 eggs, beaten
4 tablespoons grated Parmesan cheese

1/2 cup grated mozzarella cheese
1 cup diced pepperoni
Garlic salt & pepper to taste

Bread and Filling:
Add lukewarm water and flour to sourdough starter. Mix well and cover. Let stand in a warm place overnight. The next morning heat milk; then stir in butter or margarine, sugar and salt. Cool to lukewarm. Sprinkle yeast over 1/4 cup warm water. Let stand 5 minutes. Stir yeast into cooled mixture. Add to starter mixture. Mix well. Beat in 2 cups of flour until batter is smooth. Cover and let dough rise in warm place 30 to 40 minutes or until almost doubled in size. Stir down dough. Gradually beat in remaining flour until dough is stiff enough to clean sides of bowl. Turn out onto floured surface and knead dough about 5 minutes until smooth and elastic, adding more flour if necessary. Divide dough in half. Let rest, covered with cloth, for 10 minutes. Roll dough out into a rectangular shape, approximately 10" x 12". Combine filling ingredients. Spread filling on top of dough. Roll up jelly-roll style and place on a baking sheet. Brush with egg yolk. Set in warm place free from drafts and let rise until doubled in size. Bake at 375°F (191°C) for 20 minutes or until done. Makes 2 loaves.

Potato-Bacon Sourdough Bread

Glorify those leftover mashed potatoes.

2 tablespoons or 2 pkgs. dry yeast
1/2 cup lukewarm water
1 cup sourdough starter
2 cups water
2 cups grated sharp or longhorn cheese
1/2 teaspoon baking powder

2 tablespoons cooking oil or melted margarine
2 tablespoons sugar
2 tablespoons salt
1/2 cup crisply fried bacon bits
2 cups cooked mashed potatoes
6-1/2 to 7-1/2 cups all-purpose flour

Dissolve yeast in 1/2 cup lukewarm water. To sourdough starter add 2 cups water, cheese, baking powder, oil or melted margarine, sugar, salt, bacon and mashed potatoes. Add dissolved yeast and gradually beat in flour 1/2 cup at a time, stirring well after each addition. Turn out onto floured surface and knead until smooth and elastic, adding more flour if necessary. Place dough in a greased bowl, turning once. Cover with a cloth. Set in warm place free from drafts and let rise until doubled in size. Punch dough down. Shape into 2 loaves, put in greased loaf pans, cover and let rise in a warm place about 2 hours or until doubled in size. Bake at 375°F (191°C) for 40 minutes or until done. Makes 2 loaves.

Tomato-Cheese Sourdough Bread

Use canned tomatoes to make this combination.

1 cup sourdough starter
1 (28-oz.) can tomatoes, undrained
2 tablespoons or 2 pkgs. dry yeast
1/4 cup warm water (110°F, 43°C)
3/4 to 1 lb. grated sharp or longhorn cheese

1/2 teaspoon baking powder
2 to 3 tablespoons cooking oil or melted margarine
2 tablespoons sugar
2 tablespoons salt
6-1/2 to 7-1/2 cups all-purpose flour

Measure starter into a large bowl. Add canned tomatoes that have been cut into pieces or mashed, include liquid. Dissolve yeast in lukewarm water. Add cheese, baking powder, oil or melted margarine, sugar and salt to starter-tomato mixture. Add dissolved yeast and gradually beat in flour 1/2 cup at a time. Dough will be fairly thick. Turn out onto floured surface and knead 5 to 10 minutes, adding more flour if necessary. Put in a greased bowl, turning once to oil top. Cover with a cloth. Set in a warm place free from drafts and let rise until doubled in size. Punch dough down. Shape into 2 loaves and let rise about 2 hours or until doubled in size. Bake in well greased pans at 375°F (191°C) for 40 minutes or until done. Makes 2 loaves.

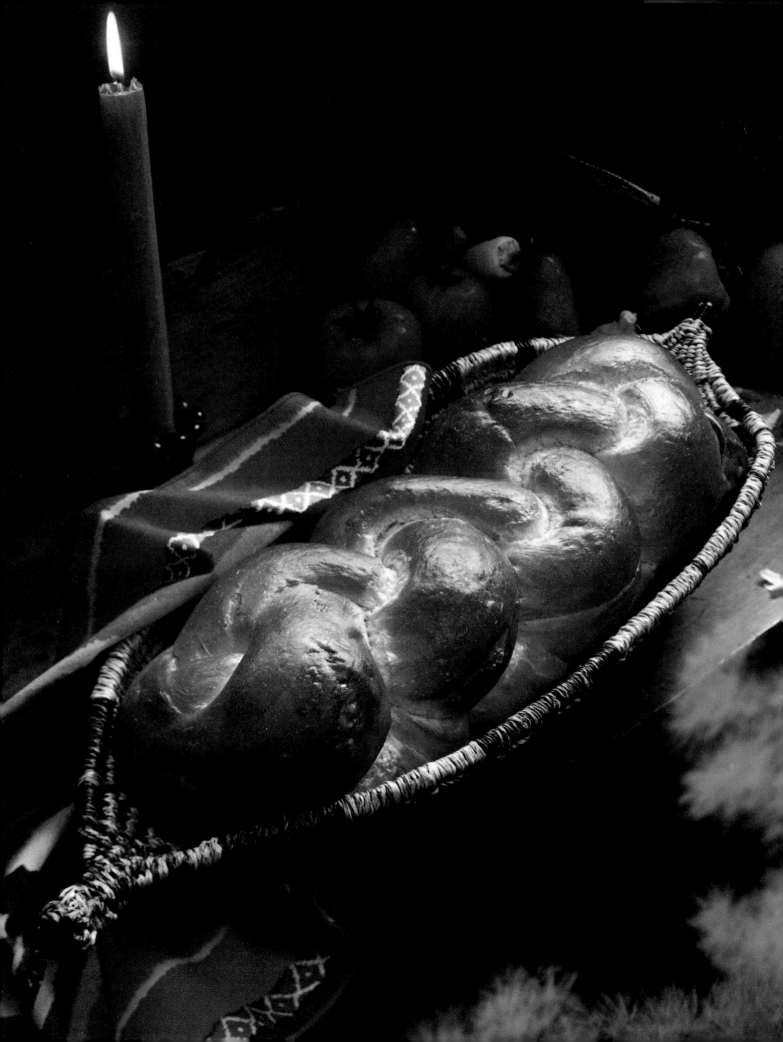

Sourdough Taco Twist

A good companion to hearty food and drink.

1 cup sourdough starter
1 cup lukewarm water
2-1/2 cups all-purpose flour

1-1/2 teaspoons salt
1/4 cup cooking oil
1 (1-oz.) pkg. sour-cream sauce mix

Filling:
1/4 cup butter or margarine, melted
1 tablespoon Taco Seasoning Mix
1/4 cup instant minced onion or
   1/2 cup finely chopped onion

1 tablespoon grated Parmesan cheese
1 teaspoon paprika

Mix together the night before 1 cup sourdough starter with 1 cup lukewarm water and 1 cup flour. Let set at least 10 hours, covered, in a large mixing bowl. Next day, grease a large cookie sheet. Add salt, oil and sour-cream-sauce mix to sourdough starter mixture. Mix well. By hand stir in remaining flour to form a soft dough. Turn out onto floured surface and knead until smooth and elastic. Roll out dough to form a 12" x 16" rectangle. Cut lengthwise into three 4" x 16" strips. Spread filling down center of each strip. Starting with longer side, roll up each strip. Seal edges and ends. On prepared cookie sheet, braid 3 rolls together. Cover with a cloth. Set in warm place free from drafts and let rise 50 to 60 minutes or until doubled in size. Bake at 350°F (177°C) for 30 to 35 minutes or until golden brown. Serve warm or cool. Makes 1 large twist.

Filling:
Combine ingredients and mix well. Set aside until needed.

Sourdough Pizza Bread

That's Italian?

1/2 cup lukewarm milk
1 cup sourdough starter
2 tablespoons sugar
1 teaspoon salt
1 egg, beaten
2 tablespoons melted butter or margarine

1/4 teaspoon garlic powder
1/2 teaspoon dried oregano, crushed
1/4 cup finely chopped pepperoni
2 to 3 cups all-purpose flour
Melted butter

Stir lukewarm milk into the sourdough starter. Add sugar, salt, egg, butter or margarine, garlic powder, oregano and pepperoni. Beat 3 minutes by hand, scraping side of bowl constantly. By hand, stir in flour, 1/2 cup at a time. Stir after each addition. Add enough flour until dough has begun to leave the sides of the bowl. Cover with a cloth. Set in warm place free from drafts and let rise for 1 hour. Stir down. Spread evenly in a greased loaf pan. Brush top with melted butter. Cover with a cloth. Set in warm place and let rise for 2 hours. Bake at 375°F (191°C) for 30 minutes. If bread starts to brown too quickly, cover with a tent of aluminum foil. Makes 1 loaf.

Sourdough Taco Twist

Sourdough Onion Twist

Cheese, onion and sesame seeds make this bread impressive in appearance and taste.

1 pkg. dry yeast	1/2 cup warm water (110°F, 43°C)
1/4 cup warm water (110°F, 43°C)	1/4 cup sugar
1 cup sourdough starter	1-1/2 teaspoons salt
1/2 cup butter or margarine, melted	1 egg, beaten
1/2 cup milk	4-1/2 to 5-1/2 cups all-purpose flour

Filling:

1 cup finely chopped onion	1 tablespoon sesame seeds
or 1/3 cup dried onion	1 teaspoon garlic salt
1/4 cup butter, melted	1 teaspoon paprika
1-1/2 tablespoons grated Parmesan cheese	

In a large mixing bowl, mix yeast and 1/4 cup warm water. Let stand 10 minutes. Add sourdough starter, butter or margarine, milk, 1/2 cup warm water, sugar, salt and beaten egg. Stir in 2 cups flour, blend at low speed until moistened. Beat 2 minutes at medium speed. Gradually stir in remaining flour until dough pulls away from side of mixing bowl. Cover with a cloth. Set in warm place free from drafts and let rise about 1 hour or until doubled in size. While dough is rising, mix all filling ingredients. Set aside. Stir down dough. Turn out onto well floured surface and knead lightly for 2 to 3 minutes, adding more flour if necessary. Roll out dough to a 12" x 18" rectangle. Cut lengthwise into three 4" x 18" strips. Spread on filling. Starting with 18" side, roll each strip around filling—jelly roll style. Seal edges and ends by pinching together. Place strips on greased cookie sheet. Press strips together at one end. Braid, keeping seams inside the braid whenever possible. Cover with a cloth and let rise in warm place free from drafts for 1 to 2 hours or until doubled in size. Bake at 350°F (177°C) for 30 minutes or until golden brown. Remove; brush with melted butter. Makes 1 large loaf.

Sourdough Onion Bread

Sprinkle with grated Cheddar cheese, toast and float a slice on steaming French onion soup.

1 cup sourdough starter	1/2 teaspoon baking powder
2 tablespoons or 2 pkgs. dry yeast	2 tablespoons cooking oil or melted margarine
1/4 cup warm water (105° to 110°F)	2 tablespoons sugar
2 cups water or scalded milk	1 pkg. dry onion-soup mix
3/4 to 1 lb. grated sharp or longhorn cheese	6 to 7 cups all-purpose flour

Measure starter into a large bowl. Dissolve yeast in 1/4 cup lukewarm water. Add 2 cups water or milk, cheese, baking powder, oil or melted margarine, sugar and onion-soup mix to sourdough starter. Add dissolved yeast and gradually beat in flour 1/2 cup at a time. Dough should be fairly stiff and pull away from sides of bowl. Turn out onto floured surface and knead, adding more flour if necessary. Put in a greased bowl, turning once. Cover with a cloth. Set in warm place free from drafts and let rise until doubled in size. Punch dough down. Shape into 2 loaves and place in well greased pans. Cover and let rise about 2 hours or until doubled in size. Bake at 375°F (191°C) for 40 minutes or until done. Makes 2 loaves.

Sourdough Sweet 'N Spicy Raisin Bread

Make this braided loaf for a special brunch.

2 cups sourdough starter
1/2 cup lukewarm milk
1/4 cup brown sugar, firmly packed
1/4 cup butter, melted
1-1/2 teaspoons salt
1 egg, slightly beaten
3 cups all-purpose flour

2 teaspoons cinnamon
1/2 teaspoon nutmeg
1-1/2 cups raisins
1/2 cup chopped nuts (optional)
2 tablespoons butter, melted
1 egg white beaten
1 tablespoon granulated sugar

Measure out sourdough starter. Add milk, brown sugar, butter, salt and egg. Mix well. Sift flour, cinnamon and nutmeg together. Combine with sourdough starter and blend well. Add raisins and nuts, if desired, Turn out onto a lightly floured surface and knead until smooth and elastic, adding more flour if necessary. Place in a greased bowl, turning once. Cover with a cloth. Set in a warm place free from drafts and let rise about 2 hours. Cut off one-third of dough and divide remaining dough into three 12-inch rolls. Place on a greased cookie sheet and braid. Pinch ends together. Make smaller braid with extra dough and place on top of large braid. Brush with melted butter. Let rise about 1 hour. Brush with beaten egg white and sprinkle with sugar. Bake at 350°F (177°C) for 40 minutes or until golden brown. Makes 1 braided loaf.

Sourdough Raisin Casserole Bread

For variety, cinnamon and nuts may be replaced by other fruits and spices.

1 cup sourdough starter
1/4 cup lukewarm milk
1/2 cup sugar
1/4 cup butter or margarine, melted
1 teaspoon salt

1 egg, beaten
1-1/2 teaspoons cinnamon
1/2 cup chopped nuts
1 cup seedless raisins
2 cups all-purpose flour

Measure out sourdough starter into large mixing bowl. Add milk sugar, butter, salt, egg, cinnamon and nuts. Combine raisins and flour. Add to batter gradually while stirring to form a stiff dough. Cover with a cloth. Set in warm place free from drafts and let rise about 1 hour or until doubled in size. Stir batter down. Place in greased 1-quart casserole dish. Bake at 350°F (177°C) for 40 to 45 minutes or until golden brown. Makes 1 loaf.

Sourdough Rocky Road Loaf

The same flavor treat, but beats cold ice cream on a winter's night.

1 cup sourdough starter
1 teaspoon dry yeast
1/4 cup lukewarm water
1/2 cup lukewarm milk
1/4 cup granulated sugar
1 teaspoon salt
1 egg
3 tablespoons cooking oil

3 cups all-purpose flour
4 tablespoons butter, softened
1/3 cup granulated sugar
1/3 cup brown sugar, firmly packed
2 teaspoons cinnamon
2/3 cup chopped nuts
2/3 cup semi-sweet chocolate chips
1 cup miniature marshmallows

Measure out sourdough starter in a large mixing bowl. Dissolve yeast in lukewarm water. Add to sourdough along with milk, 1/4 cup granulated sugar, salt, egg and shortening. Mix well. Add enough flour until the dough pulls away from the side of the bowl. Turn out onto floured surface and knead until smooth and elastic, about 5 minutes. Place in greased bowl, turning once. Cover with a cloth and let rise in a warm place free from drafts, about 1 to 2 hours or until doubled in size. Punch down dough, roll out to 1/2-inch thickness in a 14" x 10" rectangle. Spread with softened butter. Mix 1/3 cup granulated sugar, brown sugar and cinnamon together. Sprinkle over butter along with nuts, chocolate chips and marshmallows. Roll up jelly-roll style, seal edges, and shape into a loaf. Place in a well greased loaf pan, cover with a cloth and allow to rise 1 to 2 hours. Bake at 375°F (191°C) for 40 to 50 minutes or until done. Allow to cool in pan for 5 minutes before removing. Makes 1 loaf.

Quick Breads

Actually any bread that is not leavened with yeast is considered a quick bread. That includes biscuits, muffins, griddle cakes, waffles and other bread products that use either steam or a chemical such as baking powder for leavening. In this section, we use both sourdough and leaveners such as baking soda or baking powder to produce easy-to-make treats guaranteed to make any ordinary meal come alive.

Don't worry about a crack down the center of a nut bread or fruit bread. It is characteristic of this type of baking.

These breads will mellow and slice easier if thoroughly cooled and then wrapped in aluminum foil or plastic wrap, or placed in an air-tight container for several hours.

If you prefer bread served hot with butter or a cream-cheese spread, warm the bread in an oven at 300°F–350°F (149°C–177°C) for about 5 minutes. Also, most fruit breads and nut breads are delicious served toasted for breakfast. They make great sandwiches for those occasions when you feel like showing off.

Double a recipe and make an extra loaf as a nice gift for a special friend. Or freeze a loaf to be warmed and served later when a busy schedule doesn't allow any time for baking.

There are several ways to tell when quick breads are done. Insert a toothpick or straw. If it comes out free of dough, the bread is done. Another way is to press gently on the middle of the bread. If it feels firm, it's done. With some of these breads, a crack will form along the center of the loaf. By looking down into the crack, you can judge the degree of doneness. If you see raw-looking dough, obviously the loaf is not fully baked. With some recipes, you will notice that the bread has pulled away from the sides of the pan, when it's done.

Easy Sourdough Pumpkin Loaves

The golden glaze gives these loaves a beautiful topping.

Bread:

2 cups biscuit mix
1/2 cup sugar
1 teaspoon cinnamon
1/4 teaspoon allspice
1/4 teaspoon cloves
1/2 cup sourdough starter

1/2 cup canned pumpkin
1/2 cup raisins
1 egg, beaten
3/4 cup milk
2 tablespoons cooking oil

Golden Glaze:

2 cups powdered sugar
2 tablespoons light cream
Few drops yellow food coloring

Bread:

Stir together biscuit mix, sugar, cinnamon, allspice and cloves. Combine sourdough starter with pumpkin, raisins, egg, milk and salad oil. Add to dry ingredients. Stir just until blended. Turn into three greased 5-1/2" x 3" x 2" pans or one 9-1/4" x 5-1/4" x 3" loaf pan. Bake at 350°F (177°C) for 35 to 40 minutes or 50 to 55 minutes for a large loaf. Cool for 5 minutes. Remove from pan. Cool and spread with Golden Glaze. Makes 1 large loaf or 3 smaller loaves.

Golden Glaze:

Combine sugar, cream and food coloring. Spread on cooled pumpkin loaves. Halve recipe to glaze 1 large loaf.

Ginger Cheese Spread

Delicious served with Sourdough Pumpkin Bread or Pumpkin Carrot Bread.

1 (3-oz.) pkg. cream cheese
2 tablespoons milk

1 teaspoon chopped crystallized ginger
1-1/2 tablespoons chopped almonds

Soften cream cheese. Blend with other ingredients. Delicious served with Pumpkin Bread or Carrot Bread. Makes 3/4 cup.

Sourdough Pumpkin-Nut Bread

Slice and serve warm with softened butter or softened cream cheese.

1 cup brown sugar, firmly packed
1/3 cup shortening
1-1/2 cups sourdough starter
2 eggs
1 cup canned pumpkin
1/4 cup milk
1 cup all-purpose flour

1/2 teaspoon salt
1/2 teaspoon ginger
1/4 teaspoon cloves
1 teaspoon baking powder
1/2 teaspoon baking soda
1 cup chopped nuts

Cream together brown sugar and shortening until mixture is light and fluffy. Add sourdough starter. Add eggs, one at a time, beating well after each addition. Stir in pumpkin and milk. Sift together dry ingredients and stir into pumpkin mixture. Beat 1 minute with electric or rotary mixer. Stir in nuts. Bake in a greased and floured loaf pan at 350°F (177°C) for 1 hour 15 minutes or until done. Cool 5 minutes before removing from pan. Slice and serve warm with butter or softened cream cheese. Makes 1 loaf.

Note:
This bread will be very moist.

Sourdough Pumpkin-Mincemeat Bread

Delicious as a gift for the Holidays.

4 cups all-purpose flour
1-1/2 cups sugar
2 tablespoons pumpkin-pie spice
2 teaspoons baking soda
1-1/2 teaspoons salt
1-1/2 cups brown sugar, firmly packed
4 eggs, beaten

2/3 cup water
1/2 cup sourdough starter
1 cup cooking oil
2 cups canned pumpkin
1-1/2 cups prepared mincemeat
1 cup chopped nuts

In a large mixing bowl mix together flour, sugar, spice, baking soda, salt and brown sugar. Make a well in the center. Mix together eggs, water, sourdough starter, oil and pumpkin. Add all at once to well in dry ingredients. Mix well. Blend in mincemeat and nuts. Pour into 3 greased loaf pans. Bake at 350°F (177°C) for 1 hour or until done. Makes 3 loaves.

Sourdough Oatmeal-Apple Loaf

A tastier way to get your apple a day.

Bread:

1-1/2 cups sugar
1/2 cup shortening
2 eggs
1 cup sourdough starter
1/2 cup milk
1 teaspoon vanilla
2/3 cup oats
2 cups shredded apple, with peel

1 cup all-purpose flour
1-1/2 teaspoon cinnamon
1/4 teaspoon cloves
1/4 teaspoon nutmeg
1/2 teaspoon salt
1 teaspoon baking soda
3/4 cup chopped pecans

Glaze:

2/3 cup powdered sugar
1 tablespoon milk

Bread:

Cream together sugar and shortening. Add eggs and beat well. Add sourdough starter, milk and vanilla. Beat 1 minute at medium speed. Fold in oats and apple. Sift together dry ingredients. Add to sourdough mixture and mix well. Fold in chopped nuts. Bake in a well greased loaf pan at 350°F (177°C) for 50 minutes or until done. Remove from pan. Cool 10 minutes and add glaze if desired. Makes 1 loaf.

Glaze:

Mix powdered sugar and milk. Spread over bread.

Sourdough Cranberry Fruit Nut Bread

This bread uses canned cranberry sauce so you can make it anytime.

1 cup sourdough starter
1/4 cup cooking oil
1 teaspoon grated orange peel
3/4 cup orange juice
1 egg, well beaten

3/4 cup sugar
1 cup whole cranberry sauce
1-1/4 cups all-purpose flour
1/2 teaspoon baking soda
1/2 cup chopped nuts

Measure sourdough starter into a large mixing bowl. Add oil, orange peel, orange juice, egg, sugar and cranberry sauce. Mix together flour and baking soda. Add to sourdough mixture alternately with nuts. Mix just to moisten. Pour into a well greased loaf pan. Bake at 350°F (177°C) for 50 to 60 minutes or until done. Cool 5 minutes before removing from pan. Cool, wrap and store several hours before slicing. Makes 1 loaf.

Sourdough Apple-Carrot Bread

Makes a party happen.

1 cup sourdough starter
2/3 cup sugar
1/4 cup melted butter or margarine
2 eggs, slightly beaten
1 teaspoon vanilla
1 cup shredded green apple, unpeeled
1/2 cup shredded carrot

1 teaspoon cinnamon
1 teaspoon baking powder
1/2 teaspoon salt
1-3/4 cups all-purpose flour
1/2 cup chopped nuts
1/2 cup coconut

Measure out sourdough starter in a large mixing bowl. Mix together sugar, butter, eggs, vanilla, apple and carrot and add to sourdough. Mix together dry ingredients and add to sourdough mixture. Blend well. Fold in nuts and coconut. Pour into a greased loaf pan. Bake at 350°F (177°C) for 50 to 60 minutes or until done. Cool 5 to 10 minutes. Remove from pan. Cool and serve. Refrigerate any leftovers. Makes 1 loaf.

Sourdough Coconut-Carrot Loaf

For those who love coconut.

2 eggs
1/2 cup cooking oil
1 teaspoon vanilla
1/2 cup milk
1/2 cup sourdough starter
2 cups grated carrots
2 cups shredded coconut
1 cup raisins

1 cup chopped pecans
2 cups all-purpose flour
1/2 teaspoon salt
1 teaspoon baking powder
1/2 teaspoon baking soda
1 teaspoon cinnamon
1/8 teaspoon nutmeg
1 cup sugar

In a large mixing bowl beat eggs until light. Add oil, vanilla, milk and sourdough starter. Mix well. Add carrots, coconut, raisins and pecans. Mix until well blended. Combine dry ingredients and add to the first mixture. Stir just until well blended. Pour batter into a well greased loaf pan. Bake at 350°F (177°C) for 1 hour or until done. Allow to cool 5 minutes before removing from pan. Cool completely, wrap and store several hours before serving. Makes 1 loaf.

Sourdough Apricot Bread

Make ahead of time and freeze for unexpected guests.

1/2 cup chopped dried apricots
1/4 cup boiling water
1/2 cup granulated sugar
1/2 cup brown sugar
3 tablespoons cooking oil
1 egg, beaten
1/2 cup sourdough starter

1/2 cup milk
1-1/2 cup all-purpose flour
1 teaspoon baking powder
1/4 teaspoon baking soda
1/4 teaspoon salt
1/2 cup chopped nuts

Soak apricots in boiling water until plump and drain. Combine sugars, oil, egg, sourdough starter and milk. Mix well. Add flour, baking powder, baking soda and salt. Stir in apricots and nuts. Pour into greased loaf pan and bake at 350°F (177°C) for 40 to 50 minutes or until done. Cool 5 minutes and remove from pan. Cool on a wire rack, wrap and store for several hours before slicing. Makes 1 large loaf or 2 small loaves.

Sourdough Apricot-Oat Bread

Deliciously moist.

2-1/4 cups biscuit mix
1 cup rolled oats, uncooked
3/4 cup sugar
1 teaspoon baking powder
1-1/4 cups milk

1 egg, beaten
1/2 cup sourdough starter
3/4 cup chopped dried apricots
3/4 cup chopped nuts

In a large bowl combine biscuit mix, rolled oats, sugar and baking powder. In a separate bowl combine milk, egg and sourdough starter. Add to dry ingredients. Blend well. Stir in apricots and nuts. Pour into a well greased loaf pan. Bake at 350°F (177°C) for 1 hour or until done. Cool 10 minutes and remove from pan. Cool on a wire rack, wrap and store several hours before slicing. Makes 1 loaf.

Sourdough Tropical Bread

All the flavor of the tropics.

1/2 cup sourdough starter
2 eggs, slightly beaten
1/3 cup cooking oil
1/4 cup milk
1 cup mashed ripe bananas
1-1/4 cups all-purpose flour
1 teaspoon baking powder

1/2 teaspoon baking soda
1/2 teaspoon salt
2/3 cup sugar
1 cup bran cereal
1/2 cup chopped dried apricots
1/2 cup chopped walnuts

In a large mixing bowl measure out sourdough starter. Add eggs, oil, milk and banana. Mix well and add flour, baking powder, baking soda, salt, sugar, bran cereal, apricots and nuts. Mix only until dry ingredients are thoroughly moistened. Pour into a well greased loaf pan. Bake at 350°F (177°C) for 1 hour. Remove from oven. Allow to cool 10 minutes, then remove from pan. Cool, wrap, store and serve the next day for easier slicing. Makes 1 loaf.

Sourdough Pineapple Bread

A delicious blend of fruits, nuts and cereal.

1/2 cup sourdough starter
2 tablespoons cooking oil
1 cup honey
1 egg, slightly beaten
1 cup pineapple juice
2-1/2 cups all-purpose flour

2 teaspoons baking powder
1/4 teaspoon baking soda
1/2 teaspoon salt
1 cup whole bran cereal
1/2 cup flaked coconut
3/4 cup chopped walnuts

Measure out sourdough starter in a large mixing bowl. Add oil, honey, egg and pineapple juice. Mix well. Stir in the flour, baking powder, baking soda, salt, bran cereal, coconut and walnuts, mixing just until dry ingredients are moistened. Pour batter into a greased loaf pan. Bake at 350°F (177°C) for 1 hour or until done. Cool 5 minutes before removing from pan. Makes 1 loaf.

Sourdough Peach-Nut Bread

Delicious when spread with softened cream cheese.

1 cup sourdough starter
1/2 cup boiling water
1 cup chopped dried peaches
1/2 cup brown sugar, firmly packed
1/2 cup granulated sugar
1 egg, beaten
3 tablespoons cooking oil
1/2 cup milk

1/4 teaspoon cloves
1/4 teaspoon nutmeg
1/2 teaspoon cinnamon
1/2 teaspoon salt
1/2 teaspoon baking powder
1/4 teaspoon baking soda
2 cups all-purpose flour
1 cup chopped nuts

Measure sourdough starter into a large bowl. In a small bowl pour boiling water over dried peaches; soak until plump and drain. Add to sourdough starter along with sugars, egg, oil and milk. Sift together dry ingredients. Gradually add to sourdough mixture until just blended. Fold in nuts. Pour into a greased and floured loaf pan. Bake at 350°F (177°C) for 40 to 50 minutes or until done. Cool 5 minutes and remove from pan. Wrap in plastic wrap. Store several hours before slicing. Makes 1 loaf.

Orange Cheese Spread

Use as a spread for your favorite nut bread.

2 (3-oz.) pkgs. cream cheese
1/3 cup orange marmalade

1/4 teaspoon salt
1/4 teaspoon paprika

Soften cream cheese. Blend with other ingredients. Use as a spread for favorite nut bread. Makes 3/4 cup.

Sourdough Peach-Nut Bread

Sourdough Lemon Loaf

Lemon topping assures a moist texture.

Bread:

1 cup sourdough starter	3/4 teaspoon baking soda
1/2 cup shortening	1/2 teaspoon salt
1 cup sugar	1/2 cup milk
2 eggs, slightly beaten	3/4 cup finely chopped nuts
1-1/3 cups all-purpose flour	Grated peel of 1 lemon

Topping:
1/4 cup sugar
Juice of 1 lemon

Bread:

Measure out sourdough starter in large mixing bowl. In a separate bowl cream together shortening, sugar and eggs. Add to sourdough. Combine flour, soda and salt; add to mixture. Add milk and beat 1 minute. Fold in nuts and lemon peel. Pour into a greased loaf pan. Bake at 350°F (177°C) for 1 hour or until done. Pour topping over loaf when it comes from the oven. Cool 5 to 10 minutes. Remove from pan. Cool thoroughly before slicing. Makes 1 loaf.

Topping:

Combine sugar and lemon. Set aside until ready for use.

Sourdough Orange Banana-Nut Bread

A bit of orange perks up this special banana-nut bread.

1/3 cup butter or shortening	1-3/4 cups all-purpose flour
1/2 cup light-brown sugar, firmly packed	2 teaspoons baking powder
2 eggs, well beaten	1/2 teaspoon baking soda
1/2 cup sourdough starter	3/4 teaspoon salt
1 cup mashed bananas	1 teaspoon grated orange peel
1/2 cup milk	1/2 cup chopped pecans

Cream together shortening and sugar. Add eggs, sourdough starter, mashed bananas and milk. Sift together dry ingredients. Add to starter mixture. Stir in orange peel and chopped nuts. Pour into a greased loaf pan. Bake at 350°F (177°C) for 55 minutes or until done. Cool 5 minutes and remove from pan. Cool on a wire rack, wrap and store several hours before slicing. Makes 1 loaf.

Sourdough Banana-Nut Bread

Serve with cream cheese.

1 cup sugar
1 teaspoon baking soda
1 teaspoon salt
1-1/2 cups sourdough starter
1/3 cup shortening

1 egg, slightly beaten
1 cup all-purpose flour
1 cup mashed bananas
3/4 cup chopped nuts

Add sugar, baking soda and salt to sourdough starter. Melt shortening and add to batter. Add egg, flour, mashed bananas and nuts to batter. Stir until well blended. Pour batter into a greased loaf pan. Allow to sit in a warm place for approximately 20 minutes. Bake at 350°F (177°C) for 55 to 60 minutes or until done. If top browns too quickly, cover with aluminum foil. Cool 5 to 10 minutes; remove from pan. Makes 1 loaf.

Blueberry Banana-Nut Sourdough Bread

A trio of flavors combine for unique taste.

1 cup sugar
1/2 cup butter or margarine
2 eggs, beaten
1 cup sourdough starter
1-1/2 cups all-purpose flour
1/2 teaspoon salt

1 teaspoon baking soda
3 tablespoons milk
1 cup mashed banana
1/2 teaspoon vanilla
1/2 cup chopped nuts
3/4 cup blueberries

Blend sugar and butter until creamy. Beat in eggs. Add sourdough starter. Mix flour with salt and baking soda. Add to sourdough mixture. Combine milk, banana and vanilla. Mix well and add to mixture. Beat batter well after each addition. Add nuts. Fold in blueberries. Pour bread batter in a well greased loaf pan. Bake at 350°F (177°C) for 1 hour or until done. Cool 5 minutes before removing from pan. Makes 1 loaf.

Sourdough Banana Split Bread

No need to serve with a scoop.

1 cup sourdough starter
1 cup sugar
1/2 cup shortening
2 eggs
1 cup all-purpose flour

1 teaspoon baking soda
3 medium bananas, mashed
1/2 cup chopped nuts
1/2 cup maraschino cherries, halved
1/2 cup semi-sweet chocolate chips

Measure out sourdough starter in large mixing bowl. In a separate bowl cream together sugar, shortening and eggs. Add to sourdough starter along with flour, baking soda, bananas, nuts, cherries and chocolate chips. Bake in a greased loaf pan at 350°F (177°C) for 40 to 45 minutes or until done. Serve with a dollop of whipped cream, garnish with a maraschino cherry and a sprinkle of chopped nuts. Makes 1 loaf.

Sourdough Peanut Butter Bread

Two favorite flavors create this hearty treat.

1 cup boiling water
3/4 cup peanut butter, chunky style
3/4 cup non-fat powdered milk
1 egg, beaten
1/2 cup sourdough starter
1/2 cup sugar

1-3/4 cups all-purpose flour
1/4 teaspoon salt
3 teaspoons baking powder
1 teaspoon baking soda
1 cup chopped salted peanuts

In a large mixing bowl pour boiling water over peanut butter. Add powdered milk; stir and allow to cool. Add egg, sourdough starter and sugar. Mix well and blend in flour, salt, baking powder, baking soda and peanuts. Pour into a well greased loaf pan. Bake at 350°F (177°C) for 1 hour or until done. Cool 10 minutes before removing from pan. Cool on wire rack, wrap in plastic or foil, and store several hours before slicing. Makes 1 loaf.

Sourdough Prune-Nut Bread

Slice and toast for a great way to start the day.

2 cups sourdough starter
3/4 cup sugar
1/2 cup wheat germ
3/4 teaspoon salt
1/2 teaspoon cinnamon
1 egg, beaten

1/2 cup milk
1/2 cup powdered milk
1/2 cup all-purpose flour
1 cup cooked, drained prunes, chopped
1/2 cup chopped nuts

Measure sourdough starter into a large bowl. Add sugar, wheat germ, salt, cinnamon, egg, milk and powdered milk. Mix well. Fold in flour, prunes and nuts. Pour into a well greased loaf pan. Bake at 350°F (177°C) for 50 minutes or until done. Cool 5 minutes before removing from pan. Makes 1 loaf.

Sourdough Grapefruit-Prune Bread

Good flavors blended into a treat that's good for you.

2-1/2 cups all-purpose flour
3 teaspoons baking powder
1-1/2 teaspoons salt
1 cup sugar
1/2 cup margarine
1/2 cup sourdough starter

2 eggs
1/2 cup milk
1 whole grapefruit, ground
3/4 cup chopped prunes
1/2 cup chopped pecans

Sift together flour, baking powder and salt. Set aside. In a separate bowl cream together sugar and margarine. Add sourdough starter, eggs and milk. Blend well. Add dry ingredients and grapefruit to sourdough mixture. Mix thoroughly. Fold in chopped prunes and pecans. Pour into two greased loaf pans. Bake at 350°F (177°C) for 1 hour. Cool 5 minutes and remove from pans. Slice and serve warm with butter or softened cream cheese. Makes 2 loaves.

Sourdough Zucchini-Nut Loaf

A tasty way to use garden-fresh vegetables.

1/2 cup cooking oil
1 cup sugar
1 egg
1/2 cup sourdough starter
1 cup grated unpeeled zucchini
1/2 cup milk
2 cups all-purpose flour

1/2 teaspoon baking powder
1/2 teaspoon baking soda
1/2 teaspoon ground nutmeg
1 teaspoon ground cinnamon
1/2 teaspoon salt
1/2 teaspoon grated lemon peel
1/2 cup chopped walnuts.

In a large bowl mix together oil, sugar, egg, sourdough starter, zucchini and milk. In a separate bowl combine dry ingredients. Stir into zucchini mixture. Fold in lemon peel and nuts. Pour into a greased loaf pan. Bake at 325°F (163°C) for 60 to 65 minutes or until done. Cool 5 minutes and remove from pan. Cool on a wire rack, wrap and store several hours before slicing. Makes 1 loaf.

Sourdough Poppy Seed Loaf

Lemon glaze adds a tart accent to this loaf.

Bread:
1 cup sourdough starter
2 tablespoons poppy seed
1 cup powdered milk
1 teaspoon grated lemon peel
1/4 cup cooking oil

3 eggs, beaten
5 tablespoons honey
1 teaspoon vanilla
1 teaspoon baking soda
1 cup all-purpose flour

Lemon Glaze:
3 cups sifted powdered sugar
3 tablespoons water

2 teaspoons lemon juice
1 teaspoon grated lemon peel

Bread:
Measure out sourdough starter in a large bowl. Add poppy seed, milk, lemon peel, oil, eggs, honey and vanilla. Combine baking soda and flour and add to sourdough mixture. Mix well. Turn into a greased loaf pan and bake at 350°F (177°C) for 30 to 40 minutes or until done. Cool 10 minutes in pan on rack. Remove from pan and serve with glaze if desired. Makes 1 loaf.

Lemon Glaze:
Thoroughly blend all ingredients. Drizzle over top of loaf while still warm. Allow glaze to drip over sides.

Sourdough Hot Cheese-Onion Bread

Convenience foods combined and enhanced with your very own sourdough.

1 cup sourdough starter
1 teaspoon dry yeast
1/3 cup warm water (110°F, 43°C)
1 can condensed onion soup

4 cups biscuit mix
1/2 cup grated Cheddar cheese
2 tablespoons sesame seeds

Measure out sourdough starter. Dissolve yeast in warm water. Mix with onion soup and add to sourdough starter. Add biscuit mix and stir until well blended. Pour into a greased 9-inch square pan. Spread batter evenly. Sprinkle with cheese and sesame seeds. Cover and let rise 30 minutes. Bake at 400°F (205°C) for 25 minutes or until done. Makes 6 servings.

Sourdough Sopapillas

Serve with honey or cinnamon and sugar. Or, try a thick chocolate sauce for a surprise.

1 cup sourdough starter
1 cup flour
3/4 teaspoon salt

1-1/2 teaspoons baking powder
2 tablespoons shortening
Cooking oil for frying

Measure sourdough starter into a large bowl. Mix dry ingredients together. Cut in shortening until mixture resembles cornmeal. Add starter mixture to dry ingredients. Stir quickly with a fork to moisten dry ingredients. Turn out onto lightly floured surface and knead until smooth, adding small amount of flour if necessary. Cover with clean cloth and let dough rest for 5 minutes. Roll out dough into a 12" x 15" rectangle about 1/8 to 1/4-inch thick. Cut into 3-inch squares or 2" x 3" oblongs. Drop a few squares at a time into deep, hot cooking oil—400°F (205°C). Fry about 2 minutes on each side or until golden brown. Sopapillas will puff up like pillows. Drain on paper towels. Serve warm with honey and powdered sugar or cinnamon and sugar. When serving with honey, try tearing open one end or a corner of the sopapilla and fill the inside. A honey dispenser with a long, thin spout works best. Makes 3 to 4 servings.

Mexican Sourdough Corn Bread

Use cream-style or whole-kernel corn with this recipe. Try it both ways.

1 cup sourdough starter
1-1/2 cups yellow cornmeal
1-1/2 cups milk
2 eggs, beaten
2 tablespoons sugar
1/4 cup melted butter or bacon grease
1/2 teaspoon salt

1/2 to 3/4 teaspoon baking soda
1 cup of cream-style or whole-kernel corn
1/2 cup chopped onion
1-1/2 cups grated Cheddar cheese
1 small can green chiles, diced (optional)
1/4 cup diced pimientos (optional)

Mix together sourdough starter, cornmeal, milk, eggs and sugar in a large bowl. Stir in melted butter, salt, baking soda, corn, onion, cheese, green chiles and pimientos if used. Pour into a 7-1/2" x 11" pan and bake at 400°F (205°C) for 25 to 30 minutes or until done. Delicious served hot with butter. Makes 6 servings.

Stir corn and other ingredients into batter.

Pour mixture into greased baking dish.

Mexican Sourdough Corn Bread

Sourdough Hush Puppies

Serve with fish or seafood for a Southern accent.

1 cup sourdough starter
1/4 cup powdered milk
1/2 cup finely chopped onion
1 egg, beaten
1 teaspoon salt

1 teaspoon sugar
1/2 teaspoon baking soda
1-1/2 cups cornmeal
Cooking oil for frying

Measure sourdough starter into a large bowl. Add all other ingredients and mix well. Drop by tablespoonfuls into deep, hot cooking oil—400°F (205°C). Add a small amount of water if mixture is too thick to drop from spoon. Fry until crisp and golden brown. Drain on paper towels. Serve hot. Makes 6 servings.

Sourdough Corn Bread

A traditional Southern recipe that should always be served piping hot.

1 cup sourdough starter
1-1/2 cups yellow cornmeal
1-1/2 cups evaporated milk
2 eggs, beaten

2 tablespoons sugar
1/4 cup melted butter, warm
1/2 teaspoon salt
3/4 teaspoon baking soda

Thoroughly mix sourdough starter, cornmeal, evaporated milk, eggs and sugar in a large bowl. Stir in melted butter, salt and soda. Turn into a 7-1/2" x 11" greased pan. Bake at 450°F (232°C) for 25 to 30 minutes. Serve hot. Makes 6 servings.

Sourdough Corn Fritters

Use fresh corn for an old fashioned fritter like Grandma made.

1 cup sourdough starter
2 eggs, beaten
1/2 cup powdered milk
2 ears fresh corn or
   1 cup canned whole-kernel corn, drained

1/4 teaspoon instant minced onion
1/2 teaspoon salt
1/2 teaspoon baking soda
1 cup all-purpose flour
Cooking oil for frying

Measure sourdough starter into a bowl. Add eggs, powdered milk, corn and minced onion. Mix together salt, baking soda and flour. Stir into sourdough mixture until moistened. Heat 1-1/2 inches of cooking oil to 375°F (191°C) in at least a 3-inch-deep skillet, or use a mini fryer. Drop batter by tablespoonfuls into hot oil. Fry until golden brown, 1-1/2 to 2 minutes per side, turning once. Drain on paper towels. Makes 24 fritters.

Drop tablespoonfuls of batter into hot oil.

Fry until golden brown, turning once.

Rolls & Twists

Served piping-hot from the oven, drizzled with a delicate glaze, topped or filled with something delicious, these sourdough rolls and twists will attract a crowd when you want to serve something special. The delicious flavor of sourdough says welcome to busy friends and invites us to relax with a hot beverage. Whether it's breakfast, lunch or dinner, you'll find just the right roll or twist to compliment your meal.

These differ little from bread dough except in texture or softness. The structure or framework of a loaf of bread must be strong to support its weight; therefore the gluten must be stronger and well developed. Because rolls and twists are quite small in comparison, the gluten need not be as well developed. You only need to beat or knead enough to give a uniform mixture. The dough for rolls and twists is usually much softer than bread dough.

Most of these recipes are best served warm. For especially tender-crusted rolls or twists, brush the tops with softened butter or margarine before baking. If a crisper crust is desired, brush tops with milk, or with 1 egg beaten with 1 tablespoon milk. A light coating of egg white before baking gives a nice shine for a finishing touch.

I often store a batch of dough to make Sourdough Butterflake Refrigerator Rolls. I keep it tightly covered in a plastic container and it stays fresh and active for several days. To use, I pinch off enough dough to shape into a few rolls. You can wrap and freeze the dough at the time you first punch it down, as described in the individual recipes. When you're ready to use it, thaw 2-1/2 to 3 hours at room temperature or overnight in the refrigerator. Then shape as desired and allow to rise. Keep the dough covered in a warm area, free from drafts.

Also, rolls or twists may be shaped and placed on a greased baking sheet or in muffin tins as indicated in each recipe, then covered with a plastic film or foil and set directly into the freezer. After they're completely frozen, remove from pans and store in freezer bags or freezer containers. For best results, store no longer than two weeks. When ready to serve, remove from freezer about 2 hours before you plan to bake. Arrange on a greased baking pan about 2 inches apart. Cover with a clean cloth and set in a warm place to thaw and rise until almost doubled in size. This usually takes 1-1/2 to 2 hours.

Sourdough Butterflake Refrigerator Rolls

A delicious refrigerator roll with the advantage of being mixed the day before serving.

2 pkgs. dry yeast
1/3 cup warm water (110°F, 43°C)
1 cup sourdough starter
1/2 cup cooking oil
3 eggs, well beaten

1 cup warm water (110°F, 43°C)
1/2 cup sugar
2 teaspoons salt
4-1/2 to 5-1/2 cups all-purpose flour
Melted butter

Soften yeast in 1/3 cup warm water; set aside. In a large mixing bowl combine sourdough starter, oil, eggs, 1 cup warm water, sugar, salt and 2 cups all-purpose flour. Stir vigorously by hand for 1 minute. Stir in softened yeast and enough flour to make a dough that pulls away from the side of bowl. Cover with a cloth. Set in warm place free from drafts and let rise until doubled in size. Punch down, cover with a plastic wrap and refrigerate overnight. Three hours before baking, roll out dough on lightly floured surface to a 1/4 to 1/2-inch thick rectangle. Brush with melted butter. Starting with long side, roll up jelly-roll style. Cut into 1-inch slices. Place in greased muffin pans, cut side down. Cover with a cloth. Let rise in warm place free from drafts for 2-1/2 to 3 hours. Bake at 400°F (205°C) for 12 to 15 minutes or until golden brown. Makes 2 to 3 dozen rolls.

Sourdough Whole Wheat Cloverleaf Rolls

When you serve these, guests are sure to ask for your recipe.

1 pkg. dry yeast
1/4 cup warm water (110°F, 43°C)
1 cup sourdough starter
1-1/2 cups milk, scalded
1/2 cup butter or margarine

1/4 cup sugar
1-1/2 teaspoons salt
3 eggs, beaten
2-1/2 cups whole wheat flour
3 to 4 cups all-purpose flour

Dissolve yeast in warm water. Set aside for 5 minutes. Measure out sourdough starter in a large mixing bowl. Scald milk. Stir in butter or margarine, sugar and salt. Cool to lukewarm. Stir in beaten eggs and dissolved yeast. Add to sourdough starter along with whole wheat flour. Beat until well blended and free of lumps. Gradually add enough all-purpose flour to make a soft dough. Place in large greased bowl. Cover with a cloth. Set in warm place free from drafts until doubled in size. Punch down. Cover with plastic wrap and refrigerate overnight. Three hours before baking, remove from refrigerator, make 1-inch balls. Put 3 in each greased muffin cup. Cover with a cloth. Set in warm place free from drafts and let rise for 2-1/2 to 3 hours or until almost doubled in size. Bake at 400°F (205°C) for 12 to 15 minutes or until golden brown. Makes 2-1/2 dozen rolls.

Sourdough Orange Butterhorns

Sunday morning surprise.

Dough:
1 pkg. dry yeast
1/4 cup warm water (110°F, 43°C)
1 tablespoon sugar
1 cup milk, scalded
1/2 cup butter, melted

1/2 cup sugar
2 eggs, beaten
1 cup sourdough starter
1/4 teaspoon baking soda
3-1/2 to 4-1/2 cups all-purpose flour

Filling:
1/2 cup sugar
1/3 cup butter, softened

Grated peel of 1 orange

Dissolve yeast in warm water. Add 1 tablespoon sugar and set aside for 5 to 10 minutes. In a saucepan scald milk; add butter and 1/2 cup sugar. Cool to lukewarm. Add eggs, sourdough starter and baking soda. In a large mixing bowl combine sourdough mixture with dissolved yeast and 3 cups flour. Mix well. Add enough additional flour to make a thick dough. Cover with a cloth. Set in warm place free of drafts and let rise 3 hours or until doubled in size. Punch down. Turn out onto floured surface and knead lightly, adding more flour if necessary. Divide dough in half. Roll each half out on a lightly floured surface to a rectangle shape. Combine filling ingredients. Spread on rolled out dough. Starting with long side roll up like a jelly roll. Press edges to seal. Cut in 1-inch slices. Place in greased muffin tin, sealed edge down. Let rise 2-1/2 to 3 hours or until doubled in size. Bake at 375°F (191°C) for 12 to 15 minutes or until golden brown. Delicious served warm. Makes 2-1/2 dozen rolls.

Sourdough Dinner Rolls

Always the best part of any dinner when served hot.

1-1/2 cups sourdough starter
2 tablespoons sugar
1/2 teaspoon salt

3 tablespoons butter or margarine, melted
1 egg, beaten
1-3/4 to 2 cups all-purpose flour

To sourdough starter add sugar, salt and melted butter or margarine. Add beaten egg. Add 1 cup of flour and beat until smooth. Turn out onto floured surface and knead until smooth and elastic, adding more flour if necessary. Place in greased bowl, turning once. Cover with a cloth. Set in warm place free from drafts and let rise about 2 hours or until doubled in size. Punch dough down and repeat process to allow dough to double in size again. Punch down dough and shape into desired rolls. Place rolls onto a greased baking sheet. Set in a warm place free from drafts and let rise about 30 minutes or until doubled in size. Bake at 400°F (205°C) for 20 minutes or until golden brown. Makes 1-1/2 dozen rolls.

Sourdough Scones

This delicious fried sourdough bread may be served with soups, salads, main dishes or as a dessert with honey butter.

2 pkgs. dry yeast
1/2 cup lukewarm water
1-1/2 cups boiling water
1/3 cup sugar
2 tablespoons butter

2 tablespoons shortening
1 tablespoon salt
1 cup sourdough starter
2 eggs, beaten
5 to 6 cups all-purpose flour
Cooking oil for frying

Dissolve yeast in lukewarm water; set aside. Mix together boiling water, sugar, butter, shortening and salt. Cool to lukewarm. Add sourdough starter and beaten eggs. Mix well. Add dissolved yeast and enough flour to make a dough that is easy to handle. Turn out onto floured surface and knead for 3 to 5 minutes. Place in well greased, covered, plastic or glass container and refrigerate overnight. When ready to use, roll to 1/2-inch thickness on floured surface. Cut into squares, oblongs or just roll into small balls. Cover with a cloth. Let rise on well-floured surface for 1 to 2 hours. Drop into hot cooking oil—365°F (185°C). Cook one side until golden brown. Flip and cook other side. Drain on paper towel. Serve hot. Delicious with jams, jellies or honey butter. Makes 3 to 4 dozen scones.

Note:

Honey butter may be made by mixing together 1 cup honey with 3/4 cup butter and 1 egg yolk. Beat 10 minutes with electric mixer. Store in covered container and refrigerate.

Sourdough Herb Dinner Rolls

Something extra for hard-roll fanciers.

1-1/2 cups sourdough starter
1 tablespoon sugar
1/2 teaspoon salt
2 tablespoons butter, melted
1 egg

1/2 teaspoon celery seed
1/4 teaspoon crushed dried thyme
1/2 teaspoon dried parsley
1-3/4 to 2-1/2 cups all-purpose flour
Melted butter

To sourdough starter add sugar, salt and melted butter. Slightly beat egg and add to mixture. Blend together herbs and 1-1/2 cups flour. Add to batter mixture. Stir dough until it cleans the sides of the bowl. Turn out onto a floured surface and knead dough until smooth and satiny, adding additional flour. Place in a greased bowl, turning once. Cover with a cloth. Set in warm place free from drafts and let rise about 2 hours or until doubled in size. Punch down dough and form rolls into desired shapes. Place on a greased cookie sheet. Brush with melted butter and cover with a cloth. Let rise until doubled in size. Bake at 400°F (205°C) for 12 to 15 minutes. Makes 18 rolls.

Sourdough Cheese Rolls

An interesting new way to make the entire meal come alive.

1 pkg. active dry yeast	1/4 cup butter or margarine, softened
3/4 cup warm water (110°F, 43°C)	1 egg
1-1/2 cups sourdough starter	2 teaspoons salt
3-1/2 to 4-1/2 cups all-purpose flour	1/2 teaspoon baking soda
1/4 cup sugar	3/4 cup grated sharp Cheddar cheese

In a large mixer bowl, soften yeast in warm water. Blend in sourdough starter, 2 cups flour, sugar, butter or margarine, egg and salt. Beat 3 to 4 minutes with mixer. Add baking soda to 1 cup flour. Stir into flour-yeast mixture. Add cheese and enough remaining flour to make a soft dough. Turn out onto floured surface and knead for 5 to 8 minutes or until smooth. Place in greased bowl, turning once. Cover with a cloth. Set in warm area free from drafts and let rise 1-1/2 to 2 hours or until doubled in size. Punch down. Cover and let rest 10 minutes. Divide into 24 pieces. Shape into 1-inch balls. Place on greased baking sheets. Cover and let rise 25 to 30 minutes or until doubled in size. Bake at 375°F (191°C) for about 20 minutes. Makes 24 rolls.

Sourdough Cinnamon-Nut Rolls

Family members won't need coaxing to the breakfast table when these are on the menu.

1-1/2 cups sourdough starter	2 to 2-1/2 cups all-purpose flour
3/4 cup milk	Melted butter or margarine
1 teaspoon vanilla	1-1/2 teaspoons cinnamon
2 tablespoons sugar	1/4 cup sugar
1 tablespoon butter or margarine, melted	1/2 cup chopped nuts
1 teaspoon salt	Powdered sugar, milk and vanilla

To sourdough starter add milk, vanilla, sugar and melted butter or margarine. Add salt and enough flour to make a stiff dough. Turn out onto floured surface and knead until smooth and elastic, adding more flour if necessary. Dough will be soft. Place in greased bowl, turning once. Set in warm place free from drafts and let rise for 2 hours. Punch down. Roll out dough to form a rectangle that is 1/2-inch thick. Brush dough with melted butter or margarine and sprinkle with mixture of cinnamon, sugar and chopped nuts. Roll up dough like a jelly roll beginning at the shorter side. Cut roll into 1-inch thick slices. Place in a greased baking pan with the cut side of the roll upwards and with sides touching. Cover and let rise about 1 hour or until doubled in size. Bake at 400°F (205°C) for 25 to 30 minutes or until golden brown. While still warm, drizzle with mixture of powdered sugar, milk and a drop of vanilla. Makes 1-1/2 dozen rolls.

Orange-Honey Sourdough Rolls

A mouth-watering delight.

Rolls:

1 pkg. dry yeast
1/4 cup warm water (110°F, 43°C)
1/2 cup milk
1/2 cup sourdough starter

1/4 cup melted butter or margarine
1/4 cup honey
1/2 teaspoon salt
3-1/4 cups all-purpose wheat flour

Filling:

1/2 cup butter or margarine, softened
1/2 cup brown sugar, firmly packed
1 tablespoon grated orange peel
1/4 cup honey

1/2 cup all-purpose flour
1/2 cup sliced almonds
1 teaspoon orange flavoring

Rolls:

Soften yeast in water; stir in milk, sourdough starter, butter or margarine, honey and salt. Gradually mix in flour, 1/2 cup at a time. Dough will be sticky. Place in greased bowl, turning once. Cover with a cloth. Set in warm place free from drafts and let rise about 1-1/2 hours or until doubled in size. Turn out onto a lightly floured surface and knead for 5 minutes or until smooth, adding more flour if necessary. Roll dough into a 12" x 15" rectangle. Spread filling evenly over dough. Starting with a long side, roll up like a jelly roll. Cut into 1-inch thick slices and arrange cut side up, in a well greased 9" x 13" baking pan with 1-inch sides. Cover and let rise about 45 minutes or until almost doubled in size. Bake at 350°F (177°C) for 35 minutes or until browned on top. Transfer rolls to a serving board; quickly scrape out any syrup in pan and spread it over rolls. Serve warm or reheat at 350°F (177°C) for about 20 minutes while covered with a tent of aluminum foil. Makes 15 rolls.

Filling:

Beat together butter or margarine, brown sugar, orange peel and honey. Stir in flour, almonds and orange flavoring.

Sourdough Cherry Rose Rolls

Impressive appearance matched only by their delicious flavor.

1 cup sourdough starter	1 pkg. dry yeast
1/2 cup butter or margarine, melted	3 to 4 cups all-purpose flour
1/2 cup water	1 (1-lb.) can cherry-pie filling
3/4 cup milk	1 cup powdered sugar
1/2 cup sugar	1 teaspoon vanilla
1-1/2 teaspoons salt	1 tablespoon milk

Measure out sourdough starter in large mixing bowl. Add butter or margarine, water and milk that has been heated until lukewarm. Stir in sugar, salt and dry yeast. Gradually add enough flour to make a soft dough, reserving 1/2 cup flour to add during kneading. Turn out onto floured surface and knead until smooth and elastic, adding in reserved flour if necessary. Place dough in a greased bowl, turning once. Cover with plastic wrap and place in refrigerator for 2 hours or overnight. Turn dough onto lightly floured surface; divide into 18 pieces. Gently roll each piece to make a 15-inch long strand. Shape on greased baking sheet by holding one end of strand in place and wind around loosely to form coil; tuck end firmly underneath. Place 2 inches apart. Cover with a cloth. Set in a warm place free from drafts and let rise about 1 hour or until doubled in size. Make indentations about 1-inch wide in center of each coil, pressing to bottom. Fill with cherry pie filling. Bake at 400°F (205°C) for 12 to 15 minutes or until done. Remove from baking sheets and cool on wire racks. When cool, drizzle with mixture of powdered sugar, vanilla and milk. Makes 18 rolls.

Shape rolls by holding one end of strand in place and winding loosely to form coil. Tuck end firmly underneath.

After dough doubles in size, make indentations about one-inch wide in center of each coil, pressing to bottom.

Fill indentations with cherry-pie filling.

Sourdough Cherry Rose Rolls

Sourdough Pineapple Squares

A pastry-like texture makes this dessert delicious, hot or cold.

2/3 cup lukewarm milk
2 tablespoons sugar
1 pkg. dry yeast
3 cups all-purpose flour

2 teaspoons salt
1 cup shortening
1/2 cup sourdough starter
3 egg yolks, beaten

Filling:
3/4 cup sugar
3 tablespoons cornstarch

1 (16-oz.) can crushed pineapple, undrained
1 egg, beaten

Frosting:
1-1/2 cups powdered sugar
1/2 teaspoon vanilla

5 to 6 teaspoons milk

Heat milk to lukewarm. Add sugar and yeast. Stir until dissolved. In separate bowl mix together flour and salt. Cut in shortening with pastry blender until a crumbly texture develops. Add sourdough starter and egg yolks. Mix together to form stiff dough. Divide dough into 2 equal parts. On a floured surface roll dough to fit a small, well greased cookie sheet. Spread filling over bottom crust, cover with top crust and seal edges well by pressing between fingers. Cover with a cloth. Set in warm place free from drafts and let rise for 1 hour. Bake at 350°F (177°C) for 35 to 40 minutes. Cool before cutting into 3-inch squares. Frost with powdered sugar frosting. Makes 1 dozen squares.

Filling:
Mix together sugar and cornstarch in a small saucepan. Add pineapple and beated egg. Cook over moderate heat until mixture thickens.

Frosting:
Combine all ingredients, mix well. Drizzle over top of squares.

Sourdough Pineapple Sweet Rolls

Center your continental breakfast around these.

Rolls:

1 cup sourdough starter
1/2 cup milk
1/2 cup sugar
1/4 cup cooking oil

1/2 teaspoon vanilla
1 teaspoon salt
1/4 cup baking soda
3 to 4 cups all-purpose flour

Filling:

2 tablespoons softened butter
1/2 cup sugar
2 teaspoons cinnamon

1/2 teaspoon grated lemon peel
3/4 cup crushed pineapple, drained

Glaze:

1 tablespoon butter, melted
1-1/2 tablespoons milk

1 cup powdered sugar
1/4 teaspoon vanilla

Rolls:
Measure out sourdough starter in a large mixing bowl. Add milk, sugar, oil and vanilla. Mix together salt, baking soda and flour. Add to sourdough starter mixture to form a stiff dough. Turn out onto floured surface and knead until smooth and elastic, adding more flour if necessary. Roll out dough on a floured surface to form a rectangle that is 15" x 9". Spread with softened butter. Sprinkle with sugar, cinnamon, lemon peel and pineapple. Roll up dough like a jelly roll. Cut in 1-inch slices. Place in greased baking pan. Cover with a cloth. Set in warm place free from drafts and let rise 1 to 2 hours or until doubled in size. Bake at 375°F (191°C) for 25 to 30 minutes. Cool slightly and pour glaze over rolls. Delicious served hot. Makes 1-1/2 dozen rolls.

Glaze:
Blend all ingredients together, beat until smooth.

Sourdough Doughnuts

Great for sourdough nuts!

1-1/2 cups sourdough starter
1 egg, beaten
1/2 teaspoon vanilla
1/2 cup milk
2 tablespoons oil or melted butter

2-1/4 cups all-purpose flour
1/4 teaspoon baking soda
1 teaspoon salt
1/4 cup sugar
Cooking oil for frying

To sourdough starter add beaten egg, vanilla, milk and oil or melted butter. Sift together the flour, baking soda, salt and sugar. Add to batter and mix well. Turn out onto a floured surface and knead until it is slightly firm and easy to handle, adding more flour if necessary. Roll out dough to 1/2-inch thickness. Cut out doughnuts with a doughnut cutter and place the doughnuts on a lightly greased floured sheet. Allow doughnuts to rise in a warm place for about 30 minutes. Gently lift the doughnuts off cookie sheet and fry in hot cooking oil—400°F (205°C)—for 1-1/2 minutes on each side or until a golden brown. Make sure oil temperature does not drop too low. Drain on absorbent paper. Dust with powdered sugar or granulated sugar. Or dip in a glaze mixture made from powdered sugar, warm milk, a small amount of vanilla and a dash of cinnamon. Makes 18 to 20 doughnuts.

Sourdough Potato Donuts

Leftover mashed potatoes make a late treat.

1 pkg. dry yeast
1/2 cup warm water (110°F, 43°C)
2 cups milk, scalded
1/2 cup shortening
1/2 cup sugar
2 teaspoons salt

1 cup cooked mashed potatoes, not instant
2 eggs, beaten
1 cup sourdough starter
6-1/2 to 7-1/2 cups all-purpose flour
Cooking oil for frying

Glaze:
2-1/2 cups powdered sugar
1-1/2 tablespoons milk

1 teaspoon vanilla

Dissolve yeast in warm water; set aside. Scald milk; add shortening, sugar and salt. Stir until shortening is melted. Set aside to cool. Combine mashed potatoes, eggs and sourdough starter in large mixing bowl. Add cooled milk mixture and dissolved yeast. Mix well. Gradually add flour until dough pulls away from side of mixing bowl. Turn out onto floured surface and knead 2 minutes. Let rest 5 minutes. Roll out dough to 1/2-inch thick. Cut out with a donut cutter. Place on lightly floured area. Cover with a cloth. Set in warm place free from drafts and let rise 1 hour. Fry in cooking oil —350°F (177°C)—until golden brown. Remove from oil, drain, cool slightly and glaze. Makes 3 to 4 dozen donuts.
Glaze:
Combine all ingredients and stir until smooth and spread over warm donuts.

Sourdough Hot Cross Buns

Try adding nuts and raisins to this delicious, traditional bread.

Buns:

1-1/2 cups sourdough starter
1 teaspoon dry yeast
3/4 cup lukewarm milk
2 tablespoons sugar
1 tablespoon butter or margarine, melted
1 teaspoon vanilla

1 teaspoon salt
3/4 to 1 cup chopped red or
    green glace cherries
2 to 2-1/2 cups all-purpose flour
1 (8-oz.) jar stemmed red maraschino cherries

Glaze:

1-1/2 cups powdered sugar
5 teaspoons milk

Buns:

Measure out sourdough starter into large mixing bowl. Dissolve yeast in lukewarm milk, add sugar, melted butter or margarine, vanilla and salt. Add chopped cherries and enough flour to make a stiff dough. Turn out onto floured surface and knead until smooth and elastic, adding more flour if necessary. Dough will be soft. Place in greased bowl, turning once. Cover with a cloth. Set in warm place free from drafts and let rise for 2 hours. Punch down. Shape dough into 1-1/2-inch balls and place on greased baking sheet. Cover and let rise in a warm place until doubled in size. Cut deep cross in each bun with scissors. Bake at 400°F (205°C) for 10 to 15 minutes or until golden brown. Cool slightly. Pour glaze into crosses and top with maraschino cherries. Makes about 18 buns.

Glaze:

Combine sugar and milk, mixing until smooth. Pour into crosses.

Sourdough Apricot Twists

A glaze of warm apricot jam adds the perfect finishing touch.

Dough:

1 cup sourdough starter
1/2 cup lukewarm milk
1/3 cup sugar
1/4 cup cooking oil
1 teaspoon vanilla

1 teaspoon salt
1/4 teaspoon baking soda
1/2 teaspoon baking powder
3 to 4 cups all-purpose flour

Filling:

1 (8-oz.) pkg. cream cheese, softened
3/4 cup apricot jam

1 cup shredded coconut
1/2 cup chopped nuts

Measure out sourdough starter in a large mixing bowl. Add milk, sugar, oil and vanilla. Mix together salt, baking soda, baking powder and flour. Add to starter mixture to form a stiff dough. Turn out onto floured surface and knead until smooth and elastic. Roll out dough on a floured surface to form a rectangle that is 8" x 15". Spread with softened cream cheese and apricot jam. Sprinkle with coconut and nuts. From long side of rectangle, fold over twice by thirds. Using a knife or string, cut into 1-inch strips. Lift up and twist each strip as placed on greased baking sheet. Bake at 375°F (191°C) for 20 to 25 minutes. To glaze, brush with warmed apricot jam while twists are still warm. Makes 1-1/2 dozen twists.

Sourdough Sour Cream Twists

An interesting "twist" for a sweet and sour dough.

Twists:

1 cup sourdough starter
1 teaspoon dry yeast
1/4 cup warm water (110°F, 43°C)
1 cup dairy sour cream
2 tablespoons butter or margarine, melted
3 tablespoons granulated sugar

1 teaspoon salt
1 egg
3 to 4 cups all-purpose flour
3 tablespoons butter or margarine, softened
1/3 cup brown sugar, firmly packed
1-1/2 teaspoons cinnamon

Glaze:

1-1/2 cups powdered sugar
2 tablespoons butter or margarine, softened

1 teaspoon vanilla
1-1/2 tablespoons hot water

Twists:

Measure out sourdough starter. Dissolve yeast in warm water. Add to sourdough starter. Heat sour cream just to lukewarm. Add to starter mixture along with melted butter or margarine, sugar, salt and egg. Beat well. Add flour until the dough cleans the side of the bowl. Turn out onto a lightly floured surface and knead about 10 minutes or until smooth. Place in a greased bowl, turning once. Cover with a cloth. Set in warm place free from drafts and let rise about 1 hour or until doubled in size. Punch down the dough and roll into a rectangle, 24" x 6". Brush with 3 tablespoons butter. Mix brown sugar and cinnamon and sprinkle over a lengthwise half of the rectangle. Fold over the other half. Cut into 1-inch strips. Holding the strips at each end, twist in opposite directions. Place 2 inches apart on a greased baking sheet, pressing the ends on the sheet. Cover and let rise until double, about 1 hour. Bake at 375°F (191°C) for 15 to 18 minutes or until golden brown. While warm spread with glaze. Makes 1-1/2 dozen twists.

Glaze:

Mix ingredients until smooth. Set aside until needed.

Sourdough Cream Cheese Puffs

Puffy pillows of delicious flavor.

Puffs:

1 pkg. dry yeast
1/4 cup warm water (110°F, 43°C)
1/2 cup milk, scalded
1/4 cup butter or margarine
1/2 cup sourdough starter

2 tablespoons sugar
2 eggs, beaten
1 teaspoon grated lemon peel
3 cups all-purpose flour

Filling:

1 (8-oz.) pkg. cream cheese, softened
1 tablespoon sugar

1 egg yolk, slightly beaten
1 teaspoon vanilla

Puffs:

Dissolve yeast in warm water. Scald milk and combine with butter or margarine. Stir until butter is melted. Cool until lukewarm. Add sourdough starter, sugar, beaten eggs and lemon peel. Stir in dissolved yeast. Gradually add flour, mixing well. Cover the bowl with a damp cloth and refrigerate dough at least 2 hours. Divide dough into fourths. On a floured surface, roll each portion into a rectangle 1/4-inch thick. Cut into 4-inch squares. Place 1/2 tablespoon of filling on each square. Bring opposite corners to the center, pinching to seal. Place on greased cookie sheet, 2 inches apart. Cover and let rise in a warm place 25 to 35 minutes. Bake at 400°F (205°C) for 10 to 12 minutes or until golden brown. Delicious served hot. Makes 2 dozen puffs.

Filling:

Blend together cream cheese, sugar, egg and vanilla. Set aside until ready to use.

Sourdough Marshmallow Balloons

The surprise ingredient leaves its mark!

1 cup sourdough starter
1 teaspoon dry yeast
1/4 cup lukewarm water
1/2 cup lukewarm milk
1/3 cup granulated sugar
1 teaspoon salt
1 egg
1/4 cup liquid shortening

3 cups all-purpose flour
1/2 cup granulated sugar
1/2 cup brown sugar, firmly packed
2 teaspoons cinnamon
18 large marshmallows
1/2 cup butter or margarine, melted
Chopped nuts

Measure out sourdough starter in a large mixing bowl. Dissolve yeast in lukewarm water. Add to sourdough along with milk, 1/3 cup granulated sugar, salt, egg and liquid shortening. Mix well. Add enough flour until the dough pulls away from the side of the bowl. Turn out onto floured surface and knead until it feels smooth and elastic, about 5 minutes. Place in a greased bowl, turning once. Cover with a cloth. Set in warm place free from drafts and let rise 1 to 2 hours or until doubled in size. Punch down the dough and divide in half. Roll out to 1/4-inch thickness and cut in 3-inch circles. Mix 1/2 cup granulated sugar and 1/2 cup brown sugar and cinnamon together. Dip each marshmallow into melted butter, then into the sugar mixture and place on circle of dough. Sprinkle with a small portion of chopped nuts, wrap dough around marshmallow, pinching together tightly at the bottom. Dip in butter again, then in sugar mixture. Place one in each greased muffin cup. Let rise about 30 minutes. Bake at 375°F (191°C) 25 to 30 minutes or until golden brown. Makes 1-1/2 dozen balloons.

Sourdough Bagels

Popular Bagels are always a favorite.

1 cup sourdough starter
2 eggs
3 tablespoons cooking oil
2-1/2 cups all-purpose flour

1 teaspoon salt
2 tablespoons sugar
1 gal. water plus 2 tablespoons sugar

In a large mixing bowl combine sourdough starter with eggs and oil. Mix together flour, salt and sugar. Add to starter mixture. Add enough additional flour for the dough to leave the sides of the bowl. Turn out onto lightly floured surface and knead for 8 to 10 minutes or until smooth and elastic, adding more flour if necessary. Cover with a cloth. Set in warm place free from drafts until doubled in size. Turn out onto floured surface and divide into 10 to 12 pieces; shape into balls. Punch a hole in center with a floured finger. Form a doughnut shape by gently enlarging hole, working each bagel into uniform shape. Or form a strand of dough 6 inches long and 3/4 inches in diameter. Moisten the ends; seal together firmly to make doughnut shaped rolls. Cover and let rise for 15 to 20 minutes. Add sugar to water and bring to a boil. Drop each bagel into the boiling water one at a time. Boil only 4 or 5 bagels at a time. Cook for 7 minutes, turning once. Drain; place on greased cookie sheets. Bake at 375°F (191°C) for 25 to 35 minutes. Bagels should be golden brown and crusty. To serve, spread with creamy butter, dribble with honey or serve with cream cheese and smoked salmon. Makes 1-1/2 dozen bagels.

Variations:

Herb Bagels—Prepare Bagels as above, except combine 2 teaspoons dried marjoram with dry ingredients.

Onion Bagles—Prepare Bagels as above, except add 1 teaspoon instant minced onion to dry ingredients.

Sourdough Bread Sticks

Adds that extra crunch when served with any dish.

1 pkg. dry yeast
1-1/2 cups warm water (110°F, 43°C)
5 to 5-1/2 cups all-purpose flour
1 cup sourdough starter
3 tablespoons sugar

2 tablespoons butter, melted
2 teaspoons salt
1/2 teaspoon baking soda

In large mixing bowl, soften yeast in warm water. Blend in 2 cups flour, sourdough starter, sugar, butter and salt. Combine 1 cup flour and baking soda. Stir into flour-yeast mixture. Add enough remaining flour to make a moderately stiff dough. Turn out onto floured surface and knead 5 to 8 minutes or until smooth. Place in greased bowl, turning once. Cover with a cloth. Set in warm place free from drafts and let rise for 1 to 1-1/2 hours or until doubled in size. Punch down and divide into 2 balls. Roll each ball out on a floured surface to a thickness of 1/2 inch. Slice into strips 1/2-inch wide and 6-inches long. Roll each strip on floured surface with your hands to make cylindrical strips. Brush with water and place about an inch apart on lightly greased baking sheet. Let rise in warm place for 30 minutes. Bake at 400°F (205°C) for 20 minutes or until browned. Makes 1-1/2 dozen bread sticks.

Sourdough Pretzels

Men really eat 'em up. Serve some at your next party.

1/4 stick butter or margarine, softened
4 tablespoons sugar
2 teaspoons salt
1 egg

1 cup warm water (110°F, 43°C)
1-1/2 cups sourdough starter
5-1/2 cups all-purpose flour
1 egg yolk and 2 tablespoons water

Add butter, sugar, salt and egg to warm water. Cool to lukewarm. Add starter and flour, 1/2 cup at a time, stirring after each addition. Reserve 1-1/2 cups flour. Turn out onto floured surface and knead in 1-1/2 cups flour. Dough will be very stiff. Place in a greased bowl, turning once. Cover with a cloth. Set in warm place free from drafts and let rise for 2 hours. Break off pieces of dough and roll in palms of your hands until dough is approximately 18 inches in length and 1/2 inch in diameter. Twist into the shape of a pretzel. Place on greased cookie sheet. Brush with egg yolk mixed with water. If available, sprinkle with coarse salt. Set in warm place free from drafts and let rise 25 minutes or until doubled in size. Bake at 400°F (205°C) about 15 minutes or until done. Remove from baking sheets and cool on wire racks. Makes 3 dozen pretzels.

Sourdough Onion-Cheese Sandwich Buns

Makes extra-special hamburgers.

2 cups sourdough starter
1 pkg. dry yeast
1/4 cup lukewarm water
2 cups cottage cheese
2 teaspoons salt
2 tablespoons dry onion-soup mix

2 eggs, slightly beaten
1/4 cup sugar
1/2 teaspoon baking soda
1/4 teaspoon dry mustard
5 to 6 cups all-purpose flour

Measure out sourdough starter into a large mixing bowl. Dissolve yeast in lukewarm water. Add to sourdough starter. Heat cottage cheese in a saucepan until warm. Add salt, onion-soup mix, eggs, sugar, baking soda and mustard. Add to sourdough mixture. Gradually add enough flour to make a soft dough. Place in a greased bowl, turning once. Cover with a cloth. Set in warm place free from drafts and let rise for 1 to 2 hours or until doubled in size. Punch down. Divide into 18 pieces and shape into balls. Place about 2 inches apart on a greased cookie sheet. Flatten slightly. Bake at 350°F (177°C) for 20 to 25 minutes or until golden brown. Makes 18 buns.

Helen Fisher's Crouton Recipe

Delicious, flavorful, and can be conveniently prepared in your microwave, too.

1/2 cup butter
1/2 cup clean bacon drippings
3/4 teaspoon paprika
3/4 teaspoon garlic salt

3/4 teaspoon celery salt
3/4 teaspoon sweet basil
2 cups cubed sourdough bread
Parmesan cheese (optional)

Melt butter and bacon drippings in 9" x 12" glass dish in oven at 400°F (205°C) for 3 to 5 minutes. Sprinkle in paprika, garlic salt, celery salt and sweet basil. Blend together. Add cubed sourdough bread and toss lightly. Bake at 400°F (205°C) for 5 to 7 minutes. Toss occasionally until cubes reach desired brownness and all liquid is absorbed. When done, sprinkle with Parmesan cheese, if desired. Store in an airtight container.

Note:
This recipe may be used with a microwave oven. Follow directions above, except use High setting to melt butter and drippings and bake for 1 to 2 minutes.

Sourdough Cheese Taco Boats

Make these flavorful Taco Boats and refrigerate until time for baking.

1-1/2 cups sourdough starter
1/2 cup sugar
2/3 cup milk
1/4 cup butter or margarine
2 eggs, beaten

1-1/2 teaspoons salt
4-1/2 to 5-1/2 cups all-purpose flour
Melted butter or margarine
1 pkg. Taco Seasoning Mix

Filling:

3 tablespoons cream cheese
3 tablespoons butter or margarine

2 teaspoons instant minced onion
2 tablespoons chopped green peppers

Measure out sourdough starter in a large mixing bowl. Add sugar, milk, butter or margarine, eggs and salt. Mix well. Add enough flour to make a stiff dough. Turn out onto floured surface and knead 5 to 10 minutes or until smooth and elastic. Cover and let rest for 20 minutes. Shape dough into 1-inch balls. Roll out and put small amount of filling in center, fold over and seal. Brush with melted butter or margarine and sprinkle with Taco Seasoning Mix. Place in a lightly greased baking pan with buttered side up. Cover with a cloth. Set in warm place free from drafts and let rise 50 to 60 minutes or until doubled in size. Bake at 375°F (191°C) for 18 to 20 minutes or until done. Remove from pan and cool on rack. May be served warm or cold. Makes 12 to 14 boats.

Filling:
Soften cream cheese. Add butter or margarine, onion and green peppers. Mix until smooth.

Note:
This recipe may be prepared ahead of time and refrigerated 2 to 24 hours. Allow to stand at room temperature for 30 to 40 minutes after removing from refrigerator before baking.

Shape dough into small balls. Roll out and put small amount of filling in center.

Fold dough over and seal edges.

Biscuits & Muffins

Biscuits and muffins will brighten an ordinary meal with new and exciting flavors while supplying additional nutrients. Try light-as-a-feather Sourdough Angel Biscuits, colorful Sourdough Fiesta Biscuits or Fruit-Filled Muffins to turn a less-than-exciting meal into a culinary delight.

In this section you will find recipes that are easy and versatile. They give you a change of pace and bring new compliments. Keep your sourdough starter bubbling and active so you can produce tasty sourdough biscuits and muffins at a moment's notice. The recipes are truly simple, speedy and delicious!

Because gluten in the flour becomes more elastic in the sourdough batter, the texture of these breads will be a little firmer. Of course they have the aroma and flavor of genuine homemade sourdough!

Old Fashion Sourdough Biscuits

Indescribably delicious.

1/2 cup sourdough starter	1 teaspoon baking powder
1 cup water or milk	1/2 teaspoon baking soda
2-1/2 cups all-purpose flour	1 tablespoon cooking oil
3/4 teaspoon salt	1 tablespoon butter or bacon grease
1 tablespoon sugar	2 tablespoons cornmeal

Mix sourdough starter, water or milk and 1 cup of flour in a large bowl. Let stand overnight or all day at room temperature to let rise. When ready to make up biscuits, beat in 1 cup of flour. Combine salt, sugar, baking powder and baking soda with remaining 1/2 cup flour and sift over top of mixture. Mix together. Turn out onto floured surface and knead 10 to 15 times. Roll out to 1/2-inch thickness. Cut out biscuits and dip in mixture of 1 tablespoon cooking oil and 1 tablespoon melted butter or bacon grease. Place close together in a 9-inch square pan that has 1 tablespoon cornmeal sprinkled on bottom of pan. Then sprinkle remaining tablespoon of cornmeal on top of biscuits. Cover with a cloth. Set in warm place free from drafts and let rise 30 to 40 minutes. Bake at 375°F (191°C) for 30 to 35 minutes. Makes about 14 biscuits.

Note:
Serve hot. Texture hardens when biscuits are cool. Reheat by placing biscuits in a moistened paper bag. Close bag by twisting top and place in a 350°F (177°C) oven for 5 to 10 minutes.

Sourdough Buttermilk Biscuits

Try this down-home recipe with butter and molasses, y'all.

2 cups all-purpose flour	1/2 cup butter or margarine
1 teaspoon salt	1/2 cup buttermilk
1/2 teaspoon baking soda	1 cup sourdough starter
1 teaspoon baking powder	Melted butter or margarine

Sift together flour, salt, baking soda and baking powder. Using a pastry blender or a fork, cut in butter or margarine until mixture resembles cornmeal. Mix together buttermilk and starter. With a fork, stir in starter mixture until a soft dough is formed that cleans the sides of the bowl. Turn out onto floured surface and knead gently for 30 seconds. Roll dough to form a circle 1/2-inch thick. Cut into biscuits with a 2-inch round cutter. Place in a lightly greased baking pan with sides touching. Brush tops with melted butter. Cover and let rest for 30 minutes. Bake at 425°F (218°C) for 12 to 15 minutes or until tops are golden brown. Makes 12 to 15 biscuits.

Sourdough Refrigerator Biscuits

No need to wait for rising with this convenient refrigerator biscuit.

1 pkg. dry yeast	1 teaspoon baking soda
1/2 cup warm water (110°F, 43°C)	1 teaspoon salt
6 cups all-purpose flour	1 cup shortening
3 tablespoons sugar	1 cup sourdough starter
1 tablespoon baking powder	2 cups buttermilk

Dissolve yeast in warm water. Set aside for 5 minutes. In a large mixing bowl mix together flour, sugar, baking powder, baking soda and salt. Cut in shortening with pastry blender or fork till mixture resembles coarse crumbs. Make a well in dry ingredients. Combine sourdough starter, buttermilk and yeast and add all at once to well in dry ingredients. Stir only until well moistened. Place in large, greased, covered plastic container. Refrigerate. Use when needed. Remove only as much as needed. Dough should remain good for 3 to 4 days. Carefully roll out on a well floured surface to 1/2-inch thickness. Cut into biscuit shape. Place on a lightly greased baking pan with sides touching. Bake at 400°F (205°C) for 15 to 18 minutes or until done. Makes 4 dozen biscuits.

Sourdough Whole Wheat Herb Biscuits

An herbal-flavor surprise.

1 cup whole wheat flour	1 teaspoon Italian herb seasoning
2-1/2 teaspoons baking powder	1 teaspoon instant minced onion
1/2 teaspoon salt	1/4 cup shortening
1/4 teaspoon baking soda	1 cup sourdough starter
1/2 teaspoon sugar	Melted butter or margarine

Mix together flour, baking powder, salt, baking soda, sugar, Italian seasoning and minced onion. Cut in shortening with a pastry blender or fork until mixture resembles coarse cornmeal. Stir in sourdough starter until a soft dough forms that cleans the sides of the bowl. Turn out onto floured surface and knead gently for 30 seconds. Roll dough to form a circle 1/2-inch thick. Cut into biscuits with a 2-inch round cutter. Place 2 inches apart on ungreased baking sheet, lightly brush tops with melted butter. Cover and let rest for 30 minutes. Bake at 425°F (218°C) for 12 to 15 minutes or until tops are golden brown. Makes 12 biscuits.

Sourdough Cinnamon Biscuits

Easy AND delicious.

1 cup all-purpose flour
2 teaspoons baking powder
1/2 teaspoon salt
1/2 teaspoon baking soda
1/4 cup brown sugar, firmly packed
3/4 teaspoon ground cinnamon

1/4 teaspoon ground nutmeg
1/4 cup shortening
1/2 cup raisins
1 cup sourdough starter
Melted butter or margarine

Mix together flour, baking powder, salt, baking soda, brown sugar, cinnamon and nutmeg. Using a pastry blender, cut in shortening until mixture resembles coarse cornmeal. Add raisins to sourdough starter. Stir in dry ingredients until a soft dough forms that cleans the sides of the bowl. Turn out onto a floured surface and knead about 30 seconds. Roll dough into a circle, 1/2-inch thick. Cut into biscuits with a 2-inch biscuit cutter. Place 2 inches apart on a lightly greased baking sheet, then lightly brush tops with melted butter. Cover with a cloth and let rest for 30 minutes. Bake at 425°F (218°C) for 12 to 15 minutes or until tops are golden brown. Makes 12 biscuits.

Sourdough Bran Biscuits

A "bran" new biscuit idea. Healthful, too!

1 cup sourdough starter
1 teaspoon granulated yeast
1/2 cup lukewarm water
2 tablespoons brown sugar, firmly packed
1 egg, beaten

3 tablespoons cooking oil
1/2 cup whole bran cereal
1 teaspoon salt
2 to 2-1/4 cups all-purpose flour

Measure out sourdough starter in a large mixing bowl and allow to reach room temperature. Dissolve yeast in lukewarm water. Add to sourdough along with brown sugar, egg, oil and bran. Mix well. Sift together salt and flour. Add enough to starter mixture to make the dough easy to handle. Dough will be soft. Place the dough in a greased bowl, turning once. Cover with a cloth. Set in warm place free from drafts and let rise about 1-1/2 hours or until doubled in size. The dough is ready if an indentation remains when touched. Punch down the dough and with greased hands shape into 1-1/2-inch balls. The dough will be slightly sticky. Place in 2 greased layer-cake pans, 9" x 1-1/2". Cover with a cloth and let rise about 45 minutes in a warm area free from drafts. Bake at 375°F (191°C) for 20 to 25 minutes. Makes 2 dozen biscuits.

Sourdough Pecan Drop Biscuits

Try these without cinnamon-sugar topping, served open-faced with Chicken A La King, page 150.

1-1/4 cups all-purpose flour
2 teaspoons baking powder
1/2 teaspoon salt
1/4 teaspoon baking soda
1-1/2 tablespoons sugar
1/4 cup shortening

1/2 cup finely chopped pecans
1 egg, beaten
1 cup sourdough starter
2 tablespoons sugar
1/2 teaspoon cinnamon

Mix together flour, baking powder, salt, baking soda and 1-1/2 tablespoons sugar. Using a pastry blender cut in shortening until mixture resembles coarse crumbs. Stir in pecans. Add beaten egg to sourdough starter and add all at once to dry mixture, stirring with a fork. Drop by heaping teaspoonfuls onto greased baking sheet. Combine 2 tablespoons sugar and cinnamon and sprinkle over biscuits. Bake at 425°F (218°C) for 10 to 12 minutes or until golden brown. Makes 2 dozen biscuits.

Cut shortening into flour with a pastry blender. You can also use two knives, a fork, or your fingers. When blended, mixture should resemble coarse crumbs.

Drop heaping teaspoonfuls onto greased baking sheet.

Sourdough Fiesta Biscuits

A fiesta of colors and flavors.

1 cup sourdough starter
1 teaspoon granulated yeast
1/2 cup lukewarm milk
2-1/2 to 3 cups all-purpose flour
1/2 teaspoon salt
2 teaspoons baking powder

1/3 cup shortening
1/2 to 2/3 cup grated American cheese
2 tablespoons chopped pimiento
2 tablespoons chopped green pepper
Melted butter or margarine

Measure out sourdough starter in large mixing bowl. Mix together yeast and lukewarm milk to dissolve yeast. Add to sourdough starter. Mix together flour, salt and baking powder. Cut in shortening until it resembles coarse cornmeal. Add cheese, mix in pimiento and green pepper and add to starter mixture, stirring with a fork to blend ingredients. Turn out onto floured surface and knead lightly. Roll to 1/2-inch thickness. Cut into rounds with a biscuit cutter. Place on a greased baking sheet and brush with melted butter. Cover with a cloth. Set in warm place free from drafts and let rise for 50 to 60 minutes. Bake at 400°F (205°C) for 20 to 25 minutes or until golden brown. Makes 1-1/2 dozen biscuits.

Sourdough Onion-Celery Biscuits

Biscuits come to lunch or dinner and bring along a different flavor.

1/4 cup finely chopped onion
1 tablespoon butter or margarine
2 cups all-purpose flour
1 teaspoon baking powder
1/2 teaspoon baking soda
1/2 teaspoon salt

1/2 teaspoon celery seed
1/4 cup shortening
1 egg, beaten
1 cup sourdough starter
Melted butter or margarine

Sauté onion in butter. Mix thoroughly flour, baking powder, baking soda, salt and celery seed. Cut in shortening until the mixture resembles coarse cornmeal. Add cooked onion and beaten egg to sourdough starter. With a fork, stir dry ingredients all at once into starter until dough clings together. Turn out onto lightly floured surface and gently knead for 30 seconds. Roll out dough to 1/2-inch thickness. Cut with floured biscuit cutter. Place on ungreased baking sheet and brush with melted butter. Cover and let rest for 30 minutes. Bake at 425°F (218°C) for 12 to 15 minutes or until tops are golden brown. Makes 1 dozen biscuits.

Sourdough Orange-Chip Muffins

Best-ever muffin dessert for orange lovers.

1-1/2 cups all-purpose flour
1/2 cup sugar
1/2 teaspoon salt
2 teaspoons baking powder
1/4 teaspoon baking soda
1/2 cup sourdough starter

1 egg, beaten
1/2 cup orange juice
1/4 cup milk
1/3 cup cooking oil or melted shortening
2 teaspoons grated orange peel
3/4 cup semi-sweet chocolate chips

Mix together flour, sugar, salt, baking powder and baking soda. In a separate bowl mix together sourdough starter, egg, orange juice, milk, oil or shortening and orange peel. Add starter mixture all at once to dry ingredients, stirring just until moistened. Fold in chocolate chips. Fill greased or paper-lined muffin pans 2/3 full. Bake at 375°F (191°C) for 18 to 20 minutes or until done. Makes 12 to 14 muffins.

Sourdough Fruit Biscuits

A different kind of biscuit.

1-1/2 cups all-purpose flour
2-1/2 teaspoons baking powder
1/2 teaspoon salt
1/4 teaspoon baking soda
1/4 cup butter or margarine

1/3 cup finely chopped dried fruit or raisins
1 egg, beaten
1 cup sourdough starter
Melted butter or margarine

Sift together flour, baking powder, salt and baking soda. Cut in butter or margarine with a pastry blender or fork until mixture resembles coarse cornmeal. Stir in dried fruit or raisins. Add beaten egg to sourdough starter. With a fork, quickly stir sourdough starter into dry ingredients to form a soft dough. Turn out onto floured surface and knead gently for 30 seconds. Roll out dough to 1/2-inch thickness. Cut out biscuits and place on greased baking sheet. Brush tops with melted butter. Cover and let rest for 30 minutes. Bake at 425°F (218°C) for 12 to 15 minutes or until golden brown. Makes 10 to 12 biscuits.

Sourdough Date-Nut Muffins

Superb way to combine dates and nuts.

1-1/2 cups all-purpose flour
1/2 cup sugar
1/2 teaspoon salt
2 teaspoons baking powder
1/2 cup sourdough starter

1 egg, beaten
1/3 cup butter or margarine, melted
1 cup milk
1 cup chopped dates
1/2 cup chopped nuts

Mix together dry ingredients; make a well in center. Combine sourdough starter, egg, butter or margarine and milk. Mix well. Add dates and nuts. Add starter mixture all at once to well in dry ingredients. Stir until moistened. Fill greased muffin pans 2/3 full. Bake at 375° (191°C) for 20 to 25 minutes or until tops are golden brown. Makes 12 to 14 muffins.

Sourdough Lemon-Nut Muffins

Frozen lemonade concentrate is used in the dough and as a topping.

1-1/2 cups all-purpose flour
1/4 cup sugar
2 teaspoons baking powder
1/2 teaspoon salt
1/8 teaspoon baking soda
1/2 cup sourdough starter

1 egg, well beaten
1/4 cup milk
1/3 cup frozen lemonade concentrate
1/3 cup cooking oil
2 teaspoons grated lemon peel
1/2 cup chopped nuts

Mix together flour, sugar, baking powder, salt and baking soda. Make a well in center and set aside. Combine starter, egg, milk, lemonade, oil, lemon peel and nuts. Add all at once to well in dry ingredients and stir until flour is moistened. Fill greased muffin pans 2/3 full. Bake at 400°F (205°C) for 20 to 25 minutes or until tops are golden brown. Remove from pans while still warm. Brush tops with additional frozen lemonade concentrate and lightly sprinkle with additional sugar. Makes 12 to 14 muffins.

Sourdough Blueberry Banana-Nut Muffins

Your family will go bananas over this fruit combination.

1-1/2 cups all-purpose flour
1/4 cup sugar
2 teaspoons baking powder
1/2 teaspoon salt
1/2 cup sourdough starter

3/4 cup milk
1/3 cup cooking oil
1 egg, well beaten
3/4 cups blueberries, rinsed and drained
1/2 cup chopped bananas

Measure out flour in large mixing bowl. Add sugar, baking powder and salt. In separate bowl, mix sourdough starter, milk, oil and egg. Add starter mixture all at once to dry ingredients, stirring just until moistened. Fold in blueberries that have been rinsed and drained and chopped bananas. Fill well greased muffin pans 2/3 full. Bake at 400°F (205°C) for 20 to 25 minutes. Makes 12 muffins.

Sourdough Apple-Nut Muffins

Thank you Johnny Appleseed!

1-1/2 cups all-purpose flour
1/4 cup sugar
2 teaspoons baking powder
1/2 teaspoon salt
3/4 teaspoon ground cinnamon
1 egg, well beaten

1/2 cup sourdough starter
2/3 cup milk
1/3 cup cooking oil
1 cup grated apple, not peeled
1/2 cup chopped nuts

Stir together flour, sugar, baking powder, salt and ground cinnamon. Make a well in center of dry ingredients. In a separate bowl mix together egg, sourdough starter, milk, oil, apple and nuts. Add starter mixture all at once to well in dry ingredients. Stir just until moistened. Fill greased muffin pans 2/3 full. Bake at 400°F (205°C) for 20 to 25 minutes or until done. Makes 12 muffins.

Sourdough Cranberry-Orange Muffins

A beautiful color and flavor combination.

1-1/2 cups all-purpose flour
1/4 cup sugar
2 teaspoons baking powder
1/2 teaspoon salt
1/2 cup sourdough starter
3/4 cup orange juice
1/3 cup cooking oil

1 egg, beaten
3/4 cup canned cranberry sauce
1 tablespoon grated orange peel
1/2 cup chopped nuts
1/4 cup melted butter or margarine (optional)
1/2 cup sugar (optional)

Measure out flour in large mixing bowl. Add sugar, baking powder and salt. In separate bowl mix sourdough starter, orange juice, oil and egg. Add starter mixture all at once to dry ingredients, stir just until moistened. Fold in cranberry sauce, orange peel and chopped nuts. Fill well greased muffin pans 2/3 full. Bake at 400°F (205°C) for 20 to 25 minutes. Makes 12 to 14 muffins.

Optional:
While muffins are warm, dip tops in melted butter or margarine and then sugar.

Sourdough Angel Biscuits

Light as a feather, honest!

1 cup sourdough starter
1 teaspoon sugar
1 teaspoon granulated yeast
2 tablespoons lukewarm water
4 tablespoons shortening

1/2 teaspoon salt
1 teaspoon baking powder
1-1/4 to 1-1/2 cups all-purpose flour
1/4 cup melted butter or margarine

Measure sourdough starter into a large mixing bowl. Add sugar. Dissolve yeast in lukewarm water. Add to sourdough starter. Cut shortening into mixture of salt, baking powder and flour until it resembles coarse cornmeal. Add to sourdough starter, stirring well with a fork. Turn out onto lightly floured surface and knead gently, adding more flour if necessary. Roll dough out to about 1/2-inch thickness. Cut with a biscuit cutter. Dip in melted butter and place in a greased cake pan with edges touching. Cover with a cloth. Set in warm place free from drafts and let rise for 45 minutes to 1 hour. Bake at 400°F (205°C) for 20 to 25 minutes or until golden brown. Makes 12 to 14 biscuits.

Sourdough Cranberry-Orange Muffins and Angel Biscuits

Sourdough Pumpkin Muffins

Save a little bit of pumpkin from your next pumpkin pie for this tasty muffin.

1-1/2 cups all-purpose flour
2 teaspoons baking powder
1/2 teaspoon salt
1/2 cup sugar
3/4 teaspoon cinnamon
1/2 teaspoon nutmeg

1/4 cup butter or margarine
1/2 cup sourdough starter
1 egg, beaten
1/2 cup milk
1/2 cup canned pumpkin
1/2 cup seedless raisins

Mix together dry ingredients. With pastry blender cut in butter or margarine until a fine crumbly texture develops. Combine sourdough starter, egg, milk, pumpkin and raisins. Add to dry ingredients; mix only to moisten flour. Fill greased muffin pans 2/3 full. Sprinkle 1/4 teaspoon of sugar over each muffin. Bake at 400°F (205°C) for 20 to 25 minutes or until brown. Delicious served hot. Makes 12 to 14 muffins.

Sourdough Oatmeal Muffins

A nutritious muffin guaranteed to "stick to your ribs."

1 cup rolled oats
1 cup milk
1 cup all-purpose flour
1-1/2 teaspoons baking powder
1/8 teaspoon baking soda
1/2 teaspoon salt

1/2 cup brown sugar, firmly packed
1/3 cup cooking oil
1/2 cup sourdough starter
1 egg, beaten
1/2 cup seedless raisins

Soak oats in milk for 1 hour. Mix together flour, baking powder, baking soda, salt and brown sugar. Make a well in center of dry ingredients. Mix together oil, starter, egg and raisins. Combine with oats and milk. Add all at once to well in dry ingredients. Mix just until flour is moistened. Fill greased muffin pans 2/3 full. Bake at 400°F (205°C) for 20 to 25 minutes or until golden brown. Delicious served hot. Makes 12 to 14 muffins.

Sourdough Raisin Muffins

The ever-versatile raisin is at it again.

1/2 cup whole wheat flour
1-1/2 cups all-purpose flour
1/2 cup sugar
1 teaspoon salt
1/2 teaspoon baking powder
1 teaspoon baking soda

1 cup raisins
1/2 cup sourdough starter
2 eggs
1/2 cup melted shortening or cooking oil
3/4 cup evaporated milk

Mix together dry ingredients. Add raisins. In a separate bowl measure out sourdough starter; add eggs, shortening or oil and milk. Mix well. Add to dry ingredients. Stir only enough to blend. Bake in greased muffin pans at 425°F (218°C) for 20 to 25 minutes or until done. Makes 1-1/2 dozen muffins.

Sourdough Cottage Cheese Muffins

Great served with a colorful fruit salad.

1/2 cup sourdough starter
1/4 cup cooking oil
1/2 cup milk
1 cup creamed cottage cheese
2 eggs, beaten
1 tablespoon lemon peel

2 cups all-purpose flour
1-1/2 teaspoons baking powder
1/2 teaspoon baking soda
1/2 teaspoon salt
1/4 cup sugar

Measure out sourdough starter in large mixing bowl. Add oil, milk, cottage cheese, eggs and lemon peel. Mix well. Sift together dry ingredients and combine with sourdough mixture. Fill greased muffin pans 2/3 full. Bake at 400°F (205°C) for 15 to 18 minutes or until done. Makes 12 to 14 muffins.

Sourdough Pineapple Muffins

For added flavor, each muffin is topped with glaze before baking.

Muffins:

1 cup all-purpose flour
2 teaspoons baking powder
1/2 teaspoon salt
3/4 cup bran cereal
1/3 cup brown sugar, firmly packed
1/4 teaspoon cinnamon

1/2 cup sourdough starter
1 egg, beaten
1/3 cup cooking oil
1/2 cup milk
1 (8-oz.) can crushed pineapple, undrained

Glaze:

2 tablespoons sugar
1-1/2 teaspoons cornstarch

1 (8-oz.) can crushed pineapple, undrained

Muffins:

Mix together flour, baking powder, salt, bran, brown sugar and cinnamon; make a well in center. In separate bowl mix together starter, egg, oil, milk and pineapple. Add liquid ingredients to dry ingredients and stir only until all flour is moistened. Fill greased muffin pans 2/3 full. Top each muffin with a scant tablespoon of glaze mixture. Bake at 400°F (205°C) for 20 to 25 minutes or until brown. Makes 12 to 14 muffins.

Glaze:

Mix together all ingredients in a saucepan. Boil for 2 minutes. Let cool before using as a topping on uncooked muffins.

Sourdough Tropical Muffins

A good way to use up leftover ripe bananas.

1 cup sourdough starter
2 cups all-purpose flour
1/2 cup sugar
1/2 teaspoon baking soda
3/4 teaspoon salt
1/2 cup coconut

1/3 cup cooking oil
1 egg, beaten
1 cup mashed ripe bananas
1/3 cup orange juice
1 teaspoon grated orange peel

Measure out sourdough starter. Mix together dry ingredients. Add coconut. Mix together oil, egg, bananas, orange juice and peel. Add both mixtures to sourdough starter and mix well. Pour into lightly greased muffin tins. Bake at 375°F (191°C) for 25 to 30 minutes or until golden brown. Makes 16 to 18 muffins.

Make a well in the center of the dry ingredients. Add liquids all at once, pouring into the well.

Pour into lightly greased muffin tins, filling each space about 2/3 full.

Sourdough Pineapple-Macadamia-Nut Muffins

Inspired by my visit to Hawaii.

1-1/2 cups all-purpose flour
2 teaspoons baking powder
1/2 teaspoon cinnamon
3/4 teaspoon salt
1/4 teaspoon baking soda
1/2 cup sugar
1/2 cup sourdough starter

1 (8-oz.) can crushed pineapple, drained
3/4 cup pineapple juice
Milk
1 egg, beaten
1/3 cup cooking oil or melted shortening
1 cup grated coconut
1/2 cup finely chopped macadamia-nuts

Mix together flour, baking powder, cinnamon, salt, baking soda and sugar. In separate bowl measure out sourdough starter. Drain crushed pineapple, reserving juice. Add enough milk to pineapple juice to equal 3/4 cup. Add to sourdough starter along with egg, oil or shortening, coconut and crushed pineapple. Mix well. Add starter mixture all at once to dry ingredients, stirring just until moistened. Fill greased muffin pans 2/3 full. Sprinkle finely chopped macadamia nuts over tops of muffins. Bake at 375°F (191°C) for 18 to 20 minutes or until done. Makes 10 to 12 muffins.

Sourdough Pineapple-Cheese Muffins

Pineapple and cheese combine for deliciousness.

1-3/4 cups all-purpose flour
2 teaspoons baking powder
1/2 teaspoon salt
1/4 teaspoon baking soda
1/2 cup sugar
3/4 cup grated American cheese

1/2 cup sourdough starter
1 egg, beaten
1/3 cup cooking oil or melted shortening
1 (8-oz.) can crushed pineapple, undrained
1/2 cup milk

Mix together flour, baking powder, salt, baking soda, sugar and cheese. In a separate bowl combine sourdough starter with egg, oil or shortening, pineapple and milk. Add all at once to dry ingredients, stirring just until moistened. Fill greased muffin pans 2/3 full. Bake at 375°F (191°C) for 18 to 20 minutes or until done. Makes 10 to 12 muffins.

Sourdough English Muffins

Split, toast and serve with butter. My word, they're superb!

1 cup sourdough starter
3/4 cup buttermilk
2-3/4 cups all-purpose flour

6 tablespoons yellow cornmeal
1 teaspoon baking soda
1/4 teaspoon salt

Mix together sourdough starter and buttermilk. Combine flour, 4 tablespoons of cornmeal, baking soda and salt. Add to buttermilk mixture. Stir to combine well. Turn out onto lightly floured surface and knead until smooth and elastic, adding more flour if necessary. Roll dough to 3/8-inch thickness. Let rest a few minutes. Using a 3-inch cutter, cut dough into muffins. Sprinkle sheet of waxed paper with 1 tablespoon of the cornmeal, place muffins atop and sprinkle with the remaining tablespoon of cornmeal. Cover and let rise till very light, about 45 minutes. Bake on medium hot, lightly greased griddle about 30 minutes. Turn often. Cool. Split, toast and serve with butter. Makes 12 to 14 muffins.

Sourdough Bacon-Cheese Muffins

More favorite flavors join the basic sourdough goodness.

1-1/2 cups all-purpose flour
1/4 cup sugar
2 teaspoons baking powder
1/2 teaspoon salt
1/2 cup sourdough starter

2/3 cup milk
1/3 cup cooking oil
1 egg, well beaten
1/2 cup grated Cheddar cheese
4 slices bacon, fried and crumbled

Measure out flour in large mixing bowl. Add sugar, baking powder and salt. Mix together and set aside. In separate bowl mix together sourdough starter, milk, oil and egg. Stir cheese into dry ingredients. Add starter mixture all at once to dry ingredients. Stir just until moistened. Fold in crumbled bacon. Fill well greased muffin pans 2/3 full. Bake at 400°F (205°C) for 20 to 25 minutes. Makes 12 muffins.

Note:
Bacon drippings may be used instead of cooking oil.

Sourdough Mexican Muffins

"Ole!"

1-3/4 cups all-purpose flour
2 tablespoons sugar
1/4 teaspoon salt
1/8 teaspoon chili powder
1/8 teaspoon baking soda
2 teaspoons baking powder
1/2 cup sourdough starter
1/3 cup milk

1 egg, beaten
1 (8-oz.) can cream-style corn
1/4 cup cooking oil or melted shortening
1/2 cup grated Cheddar cheese
1 tablespoon chopped green chiles
2 tablespoons chopped pimiento
2 slices bacon, fried and crumbled

Mix together flour, sugar, salt, chili powder, baking soda and baking powder. In a separate bowl mix together sourdough starter, milk, egg, corn, oil or shortening, cheese, chiles, pimiento and bacon. Add all at once to dry ingredients, stirring just until moistened. Fill greased muffin pans 2/3 full. Bake at 400°F (205°C) for 20 to 25 minutes or until done. Makes 12 muffins.

Sourdough Corn Bread Muffins

Serve piping hot straight from the oven.

1 cup all-purpose flour
1 cup yellow cornmeal
2 teaspoons baking powder
1/4 teaspoon baking soda
1 teaspoon salt

1 teaspoon sugar
1/2 cup sourdough starter
1 egg, beaten
1/4 cup cooking oil
1 cup milk

Mix together dry ingredients; make well in center. In separate bowl mix together starter, egg, oil and milk. Add starter mix all at once to well in dry ingredients. Mix well. Fill greased muffin pans 2/3 full. Bake at 400°F (205°C) 15 to 20 minutes or until done. Makes 12 to 16 muffins.

Pancakes & Waffles

When preparing the recipes in this section, be sure to heat the griddle or skillet to 375°–400°F (191°–205°C). Before pouring on the batter, grease the cooking surface with shortening, cooking oil or vegetable no-stick spray. Temperature can be tested with a few drops of cold water sprinkled on the hot pan. If the drops bounce and sputter, the temperature is right. Test your pan by cooking one pancake to be sure the temperature is correct and the cooking surface is properly greased.

Sourdough pancakes have a different texture than pancakes you may be used to. This is a result of the batter sitting for 10 to 12 hours which makes the gluten more elastic. If a lighter texture is desired, separate the eggs and add the yolks to the mixture. Then beat the whites to the soft-peak stage and fold gently into the batter before cooking. The texture will still be somewhat firmer than ordinary pancakes, but sourdough pancakes are not ordinary!

Cook like any other pancakes or waffles, but cook a little longer. Wait until bubbles form and break on top of pancakes before turning. Test to find the right heat setting for your waffle iron.

Recipes included in this section range from very simple and basic Sourdough Pancakes, to the elegant Sourdough Pancake Supreme. You'll find interesting breakfasts, lunches, dinners and desserts. For added nutrition, include fruit, nuts and even granola in the batter. But don't stop with the recipes listed here. Use your imagination to create new and different toppings, and experiment with favorite foods as ingredients in pancakes, waffles and crepes!

Mix Sourdough starter with the ingredients tonight and while you sleep the starter will be busy making batter for tomorrow's breakfast!

Sourdough Crepe Suzette

A good basic sourdough crepe waiting for your special touch.

3 tablespoons butter
3 eggs, beaten
2 cups sourdough starter
3/4 cup milk
2 tablespoons sugar

1/4 teaspoon salt
1/8 teaspoon baking soda
1 teaspoon grated orange or lemon peel
1/4 teaspoon vanilla

Melt butter in a 6-inch skillet or crepe pan. Beat together eggs, sourdough starter and milk. Add sugar, salt, baking soda, orange or lemon peel, vanilla and melted butter. Batter should be consistency of heavy cream. If too thick add more milk. Heat skillet moderately hot. Pour in just enough batter to cover bottom. Immediately tilt skillet back and forth to spread batter thinly and evenly. Cook each crepe over medium heat until light brown on bottom and firm to touch on top. Loosen edges with spatula and turn. Brown second side. It should not be necessary to grease skillet for each crepe if skillet has been properly seasoned. Makes approximately 30 crepes.

Note:
Batter may be prepared hours in advance, stored in a cool place until ready to use. Crepes may be cooked in advance and kept warm until ready to serve. Crepes may also be cooked ahead and refrigerated. Heat just before serving.

For upside-down crepe griddles:
This batter must be thickened with at least 1/4 cup additional all-purpose flour to work properly with electric or non-electric upside-down crepe griddles.

Orange Sauce for Crepes

An elegant grand finale to any meal.

1/2 cup butter or margarine, melted
1-1/2 cups powdered sugar
5 tablespoons orange juice

1 tablespoon grated orange peel
Orange slices for garnish

Mix butter and powdered sugar together in chafing dish or saucepan. Add orange juice and orange peel. Heat thoroughly and pour over the folded crepes on a hot platter. Garnish with orange slices. Makes 1-1/2 cups sauce.
Note:
To flame crepes with orange sauce saturate 3 or 4 cubes of sugar with lemon extract. Place on top of orange slices. Ignite. Or add your favorite liqueur, warm and ignite.

Brandy Sauce for Crepes

A hint of brandy makes this sauce something special.

3/4 cup water
2 cups powdered sugar

1/2 cup butter
1 tablespoon brandy or brandy flavoring

Mix together water and sugar in a saucepan and boil for 5 minutes. Remove from heat and add butter. Stir until butter is melted. Add brandy. While still hot pour over folded crepes on a hot platter. Makes 1-1/2 cups sauce.

Rum Sauce for Crepes

For those who love that good rum taste.

1 cup sugar
1/2 cup water
5 tablespoons butter

1 teaspoon grated orange peel
2 tablespoons orange juice
1/4 cup rum, or 2 tablespoons imitation rum extract.

Boil sugar and water together for 5 minutes. Add butter, orange peel, juice and rum. While still hot pour over the folded crepes on a hot platter. Makes 1-1/2 cups sauce.

Note:
Complete instructions for preparing crepes in a conventional pan or one of the new upside-down crepe pans are in Mable Hoffman's excellent book, *Crepe Cookery*. This book shows exactly how to roll and fold crepes for different styles, gives you 26 additional recipes for batters, and includes 200 delicious recipes to make crepes for every occasion. Published by H.P. Books.

Sourdough Pancakes

Just waiting for your favorite topping.

2 cups all-purpose flour	1/2 teaspoon baking powder
2 cups lukewarm water	3 tablespoons melted shortening or cooking oil
1/2 cup sourdough starter	2 eggs
2 level tablespoons sugar	1/2 teaspoon baking soda, dissolved in
1 teaspoon salt	1 tablespoon water

Add flour and water to sourdough starter. Beat until smooth and let stand in a warm place overnight. Reserve 1/2 cup sourdough starter and put back into refrigerator in a covered plastic container. To the batter add sugar, salt, baking powder and melted shortening or oil. Beat in eggs. Gently fold in dissolved baking soda. Do not stir after the baking soda has been added. Cook on moderately hot, greased griddle. Do not let the oil smoke on the griddle. Makes 4 to 6 servings.

Cook pancakes on a hot, lightly greased griddle or skillet. For uniform size, use a measuring cup to pour batter. Lumps in batter will disappear during cooking.

Pancakes are ready to turn when bubbles appear on top and the griddle side is a light brown. Turn pancakes only once.

Sourdough Buckwheat Pancakes

A popular old-time favorite.

1 cup all-purpose flour
1 cup buckwheat flour
2 cups lukewarm water
1/2 cup sourdough starter
2 level tablespoons sugar
1 teaspoon salt

1/2 teaspoon baking powder
3 tablespoons melted shortening or cooking oil
2 eggs
1/2 teaspoon baking soda, dissolved in
   1 tablespoon water

Add flours and water to sourdough starter. Beat until smooth and let stand in a warm place overnight. To the batter add sugar, salt, baking powder and melted shortening or oil. Beat in eggs. Gently fold in dissolved baking soda. Do not stir after baking soda has been added. Cook on moderately hot, greased griddle. Do not let the oil smoke on the griddle. Makes 4 to 6 servings.

Sourdough Blueberry Pancakes

A good excuse to have company for brunch.

2 cups all-purpose flour
2 cups lukewarm water
1/2 cup sourdough starter
2 level teaspoons sugar
1 teaspoon salt
1/2 teaspoon baking powder

3 tablespoons melted shortening or cooking oil
2 eggs
1 cup blueberries, rinsed and drained well
1/2 teaspoon baking soda, dissolved in
   1 tablespoon water

Add flour and water to sourdough starter. Beat until smooth and let stand in a warm place overnight. Reserve 1/2 cup sourdough starter and put back into refrigerator in a covered plastic container. To the batter add sugar, salt, baking powder and melted shortening or oil. Beat in eggs. Fold in blueberries. Gently fold in dissolved baking soda. Do not stir after the baking soda has been added. Cook on moderately hot, greased griddle. Do not let the oil smoke on the griddle. Makes 4 to 6 servings.

Sourdough Applesauce Pancakes

Cinnamon and nutmeg really enhance the apple flavor.

2 cups all-purpose flour
2 cups lukewarm water
1/2 cup sourdough starter
2 level tablespoons sugar
1 teaspoon salt
1/2 teaspoon baking powder

3 tablespoons melted shortening or cooking oil
2 eggs
1 cup applesauce
1/2 teaspoon cinnamon or nutmeg (optional)
1/2 teaspoon baking soda, dissolved in
   1 tablespoon water

Add flour and water to sourdough starter. Beat until smooth and let stand in a warm place over-night. Reserve 1/2 cup sourdough starter and put back into refrigerator in a covered plastic con-tainer. To the batter add sugar, salt, baking powder and melted shortening or oil. Beat in eggs. Add applesauce and cinnamon or nutmeg, if desired. Gently fold in dissolved baking soda. Do not stir after baking soda has been added. Cook on moderately hot, greased griddle. Do not let the oil smoke on the griddle. Makes 4 to 6 servings.

Sourdough Banana Pancakes

For variety sprinkle with chopped pecans.

2 cups all-purpose flour
2 cups lukewarm water
1/2 cup sourdough starter
2 level tablespoons sugar
1 teaspoon salt
1/2 teaspoon baking powder

3 tablespoons melted shortening or cooking oil
2 eggs
1 cup mashed or sliced bananas
1/2 teaspoon baking soda, dissolved in
   1 tablespoon water

Add flour and water to sourdough starter. Beat until smooth and let stand in a warm place over-night. Reserve 1/2 cup sourdough starter and put back into refrigerator in a covered plastic con-tainer. To the batter add sugar, salt, baking powder, melted shortening or oil. Beat in eggs. Add banana and mix. Gently fold in dissolved baking soda. Do not stir after baking soda has been added. Cook on moderately hot, greased griddle. Do not let the oil smoke on the griddle. Makes 4 to 6 servings.

Sourdough Orange Pancakes

A real eye-opener for any morning!

Pancakes:

2 cups sourdough starter
3 tablespoons melted butter or cooking oil
2 eggs, slightly beaten
1 (6-oz.) can frozen orange-juice concentrate,
    use only 1/4 for batter

2 tablespoons sugar
1 teaspoon salt
1 teaspoon baking powder
1/2 teaspoon baking soda

Orange Syrup:

Remaining frozen orange-juice concentrate
1 cup sugar

1/2 cup butter

Pancakes:

Measure out sourdough starter in large mixing bowl. Add butter or oil, eggs and 1/4 cup orange juice concentrate. Keep remainder of orange juice concentrate for syrup. Add sugar, salt, baking powder and baking soda. Mix well. Cook desired size of pancake on greased griddle at a moderately hot temperature. Turn once. Serve with warm orange syrup. Makes 4 servings.

Orange Syrup:

Mix together in a small saucepan, remaining orange juice, sugar and butter. Heat to boiling, stirring occasionally. Makes 1-1/2 cups syrup.

Sourdough Pecan Pancakes

Like the flavor of pecans? Here is the ultimate!

2 cups all-purpose flour
2 cups lukewarm water
1/2 cup sourdough starter
2 level tablespoons sugar
1 teaspoon salt
1/2 teaspoon baking powder

3 tablespoons melted shortening or cooking oil
2 eggs
1/2 to 1 cup chopped pecans
1/2 teaspoon baking soda, dissolved in
    1 tablespoon water

Add flour and water to sourdough starter. Beat until smooth and let stand in a warm place overnight. Reserve 1/2 cup sourdough starter and put back into refrigerator in a covered plastic container. To the batter add sugar, salt, baking powder and melted shortening or oil. Beat in eggs. Add pecans. Gently fold in dissolved baking soda. Do not stir after baking soda has been added. Cook on moderately hot, greased griddle. Do not let the oil smoke on the griddle. Makes 4 to 6 servings

Sourdough Pineapple Pancakes

Delicious with a coconut topping!

2 cups all-purpose flour
2 cups lukewarm water
1/2 cup sourdough starter
2 level tablespoons sugar
1 teaspoon salt
1/2 teaspoon baking powder

3 tablespoons melted shortening or cooking oil
2 eggs
1 cup crushed pineapple, drained
3/4 teaspoon baking soda, dissolved in
    1 tablespoon water

Add flour and water to sourdough starter. Beat until smooth and let stand in a warm place overnight. Reserve 1/2 cup sourdough starter and put back into refrigerator in a covered plastic container. To the batter add sugar, salt, baking powder and melted shortening or oil. Beat in eggs. Add crushed pineapple. Gently fold in dissolved baking soda. Do not stir after baking soda has been added. Cook on moderately hot, greased griddle. Do not let the oil smoke on the griddle. Makes 4 to 6 servings.

Apricot Syrup

A dessert sauce to complement many types of waffles, crepes or pancakes.

1-1/2 tablespoons cornstarch
2 tablespoons sugar
1 cup apricot nectar

1/4 cup apricot marmalade
1/2 cup light corn syrup
1 tablespoon butter

In saucepan combine cornstarch with sugar. Add apricot nectar, marmalade and corn syrup. Cook over medium heat, stirring constantly, until thickened. Remove from heat. Add butter, stir until blended. Serve hot or cool. Makes 1-1/2 cups syrup.

Banana Sauce

Special for banana fans.

1 large banana, crushed
1 tablespoon lemon juice

2 tablespoons heavy cream or evaporated milk
2 cups powdered sugar

Combine crushed banana and lemon juice. Add cream and beat well with electric mixer or rotary beater. Add powdered sugar and beat until well blended. Makes 1 cup.

Cinnamon Syrup

Make ahead of time and reheat for serving.

3/4 cup brown sugar, firmly packed
1/4 teaspoon cinnamon
1/4 cup butter or margarine

1/4 cup water
3 tablespoons light corn syrup

Combine all ingredients in saucepan and cook about 10 to 15 minutes, until mixture thickens or reaches 225°F (107°C). Makes 1 cup.

Sourdough Pancake Supreme

Meringue topping adds glamour to these dessert pancakes.

Pancakes:

1/2 cup sourdough starter
1/4 cup light cream
1 egg, beaten
2 tablespoons melted butter
1 cup milk
1 cup all-purpose flour
2 teaspoons baking powder
1/4 teaspoon salt

1/8 teaspoon baking soda
1 tablespoon sugar
1 recipe of Meringue Mix
1 pt. fresh strawberries, halved & sweetened or
   1 (11-oz.) pkg. frozen strawberries
Melted butter
Brown sugar

Meringue Mix:

1/2 cup sugar
2 tablespoons water

3 egg whites, stiffly beaten

Pancakes:

In large mixing bowl measure out sourdough starter. Add cream, egg, butter and milk. Mix well. Mix together dry ingredients. Gradually add to starter mixture and beat until smooth. Heat lightly greased griddle. Cook 6-inch pancakes. Spread each pancake with melted butter and sprinkle with brown sugar. Stack 6 or more cakes. Cover with meringue. Place under broiler until golden on top. Heat strawberries to boiling point. Cut stack of pancakes in wedges and serve with hot strawberries. Makes 4 servings.

Meringue Mix:

Combine sugar and water in small saucepan. Cook until sugar dissolves. Pour over stiffly beaten egg whites, beating constantly. Use to cover pancake stack.

Spread each pancake with melted butter and sprinkle with brown sugar. Stack 6 or more pancakes.

Cover stack with meringue mix.

Sourdough Cottage Cheese Pancakes

The light delicate flavor of cottage cheese with added nutrition.

2 cups all-purpose flour
2 cups lukewarm water
1/2 cup sourdough starter
2 level tablespoons sugar
1 teaspoon salt
1/2 teaspoon baking powder

3 tablespoons melted shortening or cooking oil
2 eggs
1 cup creamed cottage cheese
1/2 teaspoon baking soda, dissolved in
   1 tablespoon water

Add flour and water to sourdough starter. Beat until smooth and let stand in a warm place overnight. Reserve 1/2 cup sourdough starter and put back into refrigerator in a covered plastic container. To the batter add sugar, salt, baking powder and melted shortening or oil. Beat in eggs. Add cottage cheese. Gently fold in dissolved baking soda. Do not stir after baking soda has been added. Cook on moderately hot, greased griddle. Do not let the oil smoke on the griddle. Makes 4 to 6 servings.

Sourdough Bacon Pancakes

Getting it all together.

2 cups all-purpose flour
2 cups lukewarm water
1/2 cup sourdough starter
2 level tablespoons sugar
1 teaspoon salt
1/2 teaspoon baking powder

3 tablespoons melted shortening or cooking oil
2 eggs
6 to 8 slices bacon, fried and crumbled
1/2 teaspoon baking soda, dissolved in
   1 tablespoon water

Add flour and water to sourdough starter. Beat until smooth and let stand in a warm place overnight. Reserve 1/2 cup sourdough starter and put back into refrigerator in a covered plastic container. To the batter add sugar, salt, baking powder and melted shortening or oil. Beat in eggs. Add crumbled bacon. Gently fold in dissolved baking soda. Do not stir after baking soda has been added. Cook on moderately hot, greased griddle. Do not let the oil smoke on the griddle. Makes 4 to 6 servings.

Sourdough Corn Bread Pancakes

Chicken A La King is one of many possible toppings.

1/2 cup sourdough starter
1 egg, beaten
1/2 cup milk
3/4 cup cornmeal
1/3 cup all-purpose flour
1/2 teaspoon salt

2 teaspoons sugar
1 teaspoon baking powder
1/4 teaspoon baking soda
1/3 cup sour cream
1-1/2 tablespoons melted shortening or
   cooking oil

Measure out sourdough starter in large mixing bowl. Add egg and milk. Mix well. Stir in dry ingredients. Blend well and fold in sour cream and shortening. Cook pancakes in fry pan in small amount of shortening. Delicious served hot topped with Chicken A La King, page 150. Makes 4 to 6 servings.

Sourdough Onion Pancakes

Make these to serve with your favorite creamed vegetable, ham or tuna.

1/3 cup finely chopped onion
1 tablespoon butter
1 cup sourdough starter
1 egg, beaten
1 cup milk
2 tablespoons cooking oil

1-1/4 cups all-purpose flour
2 teaspoons baking powder
1/4 teaspoon baking soda
1 tablespoon sugar
1/2 teaspoon salt

Sauté onion in butter until tender. Meanwhile, in large mixing bowl, mix together sourdough starter, egg, milk and oil. In a separate bowl, stir together dry ingredients. Add all at once to starter mixture. Stir just until flour is moistened. Add onions to batter. Cook on hot, greased griddle until golden brown. Serve with your favorite creamed vegetable, ham or tuna. Makes twelve 4-inch pancakes.

Sourdough Apricot-Pecan Waffles

Really yummy!

Waffles:
2 cups sourdough starter
2 eggs, beaten
1/2 cup cooking oil
1/2 cup milk
1/2 cup all-purpose flour
2 teaspoons baking powder

1/2 teaspoon salt
1/4 teaspoon baking soda
1 teaspoon grated orange peel
1 tablespoon sugar
1 cup chopped pecans

Apricot Sauce:
1 (8-3/4-oz.) can unpeeled apricot halves,
    drained and sliced
1/2 cup maple-flavored syrup
2 tablespoons cornstarch

1 cup apricot nectar
1 tablespoon lemon juice
3 tablespoons honey

Waffles:
In large mixing bowl measure out sourdough starter. Add eggs, oil, milk and beat well. In separate bowl, mix together flour, baking powder, salt, baking soda, orange peel and sugar. Add all at once to starter mixture. Beat just until blended. Spread batter on lightly greased, preheated waffle grids. Sprinkle with 1/3 cup pecans. Cook for 5 to 6 minutes. Repeat. Serve with Apricot Sauce. Makes 2 to 3 servings.

Apricot Sauce:
Drain apricot halves. Reserve syrup. Slice fruit and set aside. In saucepan blend reserved apricot syrup, maple-flavored syrup, cornstarch, apricot nectar, lemon juice and honey. Cook and stir over medium heat until mixture thickens and bubbles. Stir in apricots, heat and serve over waffles. Makes 2 cups sauce.

Sourdough Apricot-Pecan Waffles

Sourdough Waffles

Make your own variation with this basic recipe.

2 cups all-purpose flour
2 cups lukewarm water
1/2 cup sourdough starter
2 level tablespoons sugar
1 teaspoon salt

1/2 teaspoon baking powder
5 tablespoons melted shortening or cooking oil
3 eggs
1/2 teaspoon baking soda, dissolved in
    1 tablespoon water

Add flour and water to sourdough starter. Beat until smooth and let stand in a warm place overnight. To the batter add sugar, salt, baking powder and melted shortening or oil. Beat in eggs. Gently fold in dissolved baking soda. Do not stir after baking soda has been added. Spread batter on lightly greased, preheated waffle grids. Cook for 5 to 6 minutes. Repeat. Makes 4 to 6 servings.

Sourdough Gingerbread Waffles

Delicious when served with applesauce and bacon or whipped cream and sliced bananas.

1/2 cup molasses
6 tablespoons cooking oil
1/2 cup sourdough starter
1 cup milk
2 eggs, slightly beaten
2 cups all-purpose flour

2 teaspoons baking powder
1/2 teaspoon baking soda
1 teaspoon salt
1 teaspoon ginger
1/2 teaspoon cinnamon
4 tablespoons sugar

Mix together molasses, oil, sourdough starter, milk and eggs. Combine flour with baking powder, baking soda, salt, ginger, cinnamon and sugar. Add dry ingredients to starter mixture and blend well. Pour desired amount of batter on hot waffle grids. Cook about 5 to 6 minutes or until done. Makes 6 small waffles.

Sourdough Granola Waffles

Delicious served with fruit, ice cream or favorite syrup as topping.

2 cups all-purpose flour
2 cups lukewarm water
1/2 cup sourdough starter
2 level tablespoons sugar
1 teaspoon salt
1/2 teaspoon baking powder

5 tablespoons melted shortening or cooking oil
3 eggs
1/2 teaspoon baking soda, dissolved in
   1 tablespoon water
1-1/2 cups granola

Add flour and water to sourdough starter. Beat until smooth and let stand in a warm place over-night. To the dough add sugar, salt, baking powder and melted shortening or oil. Beat in eggs. Gently fold in dissolved baking soda. Do not stir after baking soda has been added. Spread batter on lightly greased, preheated waffle grids. Sprinkle 1/4 cup granola on top of batter. Cook for 5 to 6 minutes. Repeat. Makes a very crisp waffle. Makes 6 servings.

Best-Ever Granola

Store in a decorative air-tight container for a delicious and welcome gift at holiday time.

12 cups old-fashioned rolled oats
1-1/2 cups wheat germ
1 lb. shredded coconut
2 cups raw sunflower seeds
1 cup sesame seeds
3 cups chopped nuts
1-1/2 cups dark-brown sugar, firmly packed

1-1/2 cups water
1-1/2 cups safflower oil
1/2 cup honey
3/4 cup molasses
1 teaspoon salt
1 tablespoon cinnamon
1 tablespoon vanilla

Mix rolled oats, wheat germ, coconut, sunflower seeds, sesame seeds and chopped nuts together; set aside. Mix together remaining ingredients in a saucepan over medium heat. Heat until dissolved while stirring, but do not boil. Pour over dry mix ingredients. Stir well until all dry mix is coated. Spread into six 9" x 13" pans or cookie sheets with sides. Bake at 250° to 300°F (121° to 149°C) for 20 to 30 minutes. Time and temperature will depend on how thickly mixture is spread and how crunchy desired. Stir occasionally while baking. Cool. Store in covered container. Keeps for several weeks or may be frozen for future use. Makes approximately 20 to 24 cups of granola.

Note:
Raisins or other dried fruit can be added *after* baking.

Cookies & Brownies

This is probably the most surprising part of Sourdough Cookery, even to experienced sourdough cooks. You may wonder how the tangy flavor of sourdough will blend with spices, fruits and nuts. Try these recipes and you'll agree—they are delicious.

Peanut butter, applesauce, nuts and brown sugar combine to produce the best-ever brownies. Jelly gives a jewel-like sparkle to Jelly Gems. Chocolate and marshmallows help sourdough become a Goo-Goo reminiscent of my favorite candy bar—sold only in the South. Crushed candy can be used to give a stained-glass appearance.

This section offers a variety of doughs, interesting shapes, intriguing flavors and preparation techniques for you to make with sourdough. When shared with others, these treats will make the best-remembered gifts and goodies. Friends will express surprise at the delicious flavor sourdough adds to favorite cookie and brownie recipes. Whether you bake cookies that are dropped from a spoon, shaped, or spectacularly decorated, just try to keep the cookie jar filled.

Sourdough Butteroons

A delicate fruit flavor coated with coconut.

1/2 cup butter
1/2 cup sugar
1 egg
1/2 cup sourdough starter
1 (8-oz.) can crushed pineapple, drained

1 cup all-purpose flour
2 teaspoons grated lemon peel
2 teaspoons grated orange peel
1/4 teaspoon salt
1 cup coconut

Cream together butter and sugar. Add egg, sourdough starter and crushed pineapple. Blend in flour, lemon peel, orange peel and salt. Drop by teaspoonfuls on coconut and roll until cookie mixture is coated with coconut. Place on ungreased baking sheet 1 inch apart. Bake at 325°F (163°C) for 10 to 15 minutes or until light golden brown. Makes 2 dozen cookies.

Sourdough Orange Candy Cookies

Diced orange-slice candy gives an interesting taste and texture to these flavorful cookies.

1-1/2 cups brown sugar, firmly packed
1/2 cup shortening
2 eggs
1/2 cup sourdough starter
2 cups all-purpose flour
1 teaspoon baking soda
1 teaspoon baking powder

1/2 teaspoon salt
1 lb. orange-slice candy, diced and
  mixed with 1/2 cup flour
1/2 cup chopped nuts
1/2 cup flaked coconut
1/2 cup rolled oats

In large mixing bowl cream together sugar and shortening until light and fluffy. Beat in eggs and sourdough starter. Mix together flour, baking soda, baking powder and salt. Add to sourdough mixture. Fold in candy, nuts, coconut and rolled oats, mixing well. Roll into balls, about 1 inch in diameter. Place on greased cookie sheet and press down with the tines of a dinner fork. Bake at 325°F (163°C) for about 12 to 15 minutes or until golden brown. Makes 3 to 4 dozen cookies.

Note:
Dip knife in water before dicing orange-slice candy.

Sourdough Fruit Cocktail Cookies

Fruit cocktail never had it so good.

1/2 cup sourdough starter
1-1/2 cups brown sugar, firmly packed
1 cup shortening
1 egg
1 (16-oz.) can fruit cocktail, undrained
1 teaspoon vanilla

4 cups all-purpose flour
1 teaspoon baking soda
1 teaspoon cinnamon
1 teaspoon cloves
1 teaspoon salt
1 cup chopped walnuts or pecans

Measure out sourdough starter into a large mixing bowl. In a separate bowl cream together brown sugar and shortening. Add egg and mix well. Add to sourdough starter. Fold in fruit cocktail and vanilla. Sift together dry ingredients, mix with nuts and combine with other ingredients. Drop by teaspoonfuls onto a greased cookie sheet 1 inch apart. Bake at 375°F (191°C) for 15 to 18 minutes or until done. Cookies will be light brown. Makes 5 dozen cookies.

Sourdough Banana-Oatmeal Cookies

The banana for this favorite cookie should be nice and ripe.

1/2 cup sourdough starter
1 cup shortening
1 cup sugar
2 eggs
2 cups all-purpose flour
1/4 teaspoon nutmeg
1/2 teaspoon salt

1/4 teaspoon baking soda
1 teaspoon cinnamon
1 cup mashed ripe bananas
2 cups rolled oats, uncooked
1/2 cup chopped nuts (optional)
1 cup raisins (optional)

Measure sourdough starter into a large mixing bowl. In a separate bowl cream together shortening and sugar. Add eggs and mix until fluffy. Add sugar mixture to sourdough starter; mix. Sift together dry ingredients. Add to sourdough mixture. Add bananas and beat until smooth. Fold in rolled oats. If desired, add nuts and raisins. Drop by teaspoonfuls onto greased cookie sheets. Bake at 375°F (191°C) for 15 minutes or until golden brown. Makes 3 dozen cookies.

Sourdough Oat-Chip Cookies

For variety, omit pecan and chocolate chips and add 1 cup raisins and 1 cup peanuts.

1 cup shortening, softened
1 cup brown sugar, firmly packed
1 cup granulated sugar
2 eggs
1/2 cup sourdough starter
1/2 cup milk
1 cup all-purpose flour

1 teaspoon baking soda
1/2 teaspoon baking powder
1/2 teaspoon salt
1 teaspoon vanilla
2 cups rolled oats, uncooked
1 cup chopped pecans
1 (6-oz.) pkg. chocolate chips

In a large mixing bowl cream together shortening and sugars. Add eggs, sourdough starter and milk. Mix well. Stir together flour, baking soda, baking powder and salt. Add to sourdough starter along with vanilla. Mix well. Stir in oats, pecans and chocolate chips. Drop by rounded teaspoonfuls 2 inches apart onto a greased cookie sheet. Bake at 350°F (177°C) for 12 to 15 minutes. Cool about 2 minutes, then remove from cookie sheet. Makes 4 dozen cookies.

Sourdough Oatmeal Cookies

Special for oatmeal cookie fans.

1 cup shortening
1 cup granulated sugar
1/2 cup brown sugar, firmly packed
1 egg
1/4 cup water
1 cup sourdough starter
1 teaspoon vanilla

1/2 teaspoon baking soda
1 teaspoon salt
1 cup all-purpose flour
2-1/2 cups rolled oats, uncooked
1 cup raisins (optional)
1/2 cup chopped nuts (optional)

Cream shortening with sugars. Add egg and water. Beat until light and fluffy. Add sourdough starter, vanilla, baking soda, salt and flour. Mix well. Add rolled oats. If desired, add raisins and nuts. Dough will be thick. Drop by teaspoonfuls onto a greased baking sheet. Bake at 400°F (205°C) for 10 to 12 minutes or until golden brown. Cool on a wire rack before storing. Makes 3 dozen cookies.

Stained-Glass Sourdough Cookies

A beautiful way to decorate your Christmas tree. Invite the whole family to participate. Also great for gift giving.

1/2 cup sourdough starter
5 eggs
1 teaspoon vanilla
3-1/2 cups powdered sugar

4 cups flour
Beaten egg white
Lifesavers or Brach's colored candy balls, crushed

Mix together sourdough starter, eggs, vanilla and sugar. Gradually add flour to form a very thick dough, adding more if necessary. Knead until smooth. Chill for several hours. Trace picture from coloring books on foil. Grease foil or use cooking oil spray. Roll dough into thin narrow strands the size of a pencil. With strands of dough outline the shapes and details of pictures drawn on foil. Brush dough with beaten egg white. Separate candy balls into matching colors and crush. Fill in the middle of cookies with crushed candy. Bake at 350°F (177°C) for 5 to 8 minutes or until dough starts to harden. Do not brown. If cookies are to be used as ornaments, remove after 3 minutes baking time and poke holes at top. Insert cut pieces of straws to keep holes open. Return to oven to finish baking. Cool thoroughly before removing from foil.

Trace outline of desired cookie shapes on foil. Then grease foil lightly.

Using strands of dough, outline cookie shapes following traces on foil. Brush with beaten egg white.

Fill in center of cookies with crushed candy.

Sourdough Pineapple Cookies

A Polynesian yummie.

1/2 cup shortening
1/2 cup granulated sugar
1/2 cup brown sugar, firmly packed
1 cup crushed pineapple
1/2 cup sourdough starter
1 egg, well beaten

2-1/4 cups all-purpose flour
1 teaspoon baking soda
1/4 teaspoon salt
1 teaspoon vanilla
1 cup chopped nuts
1 cup shredded coconut

Cream shortening with sugars; add crushed pineapple and sourdough starter. Add beaten egg. Sift together flour, soda and salt. Add to sourdough mixture along with vanilla. Add nuts and coconut. Mix well. Drop by teaspoonfuls onto greased cookie sheet. Bake at 350°F (177°C) 12 to 15 minutes or until golden brown. Do not overbake. Makes 3 dozen cookies.

Sourdough Pineapple-Raisin Cookies

Makes great school-lunch goodies.

1 cup raisins
3/4 cup crushed pineapple, undrained
1/2 cup butter or margarine
1 cup brown sugar, firmly packed
1 egg
1 teaspoon vanilla

1/2 cup sourdough starter
2 cups all-purpose flour
1 teaspoon baking powder
1/2 teaspoon baking soda
1/2 teaspoon salt
3/4 cup chopped nuts

Combine raisins and pineapple; set aside. In large mixing bowl cream together butter and sugar. Add egg, vanilla and sourdough starter. Stir in raisins and pineapple. In a separate bowl mix together flour, baking powder, baking soda, salt and nuts. Add to sourdough mixture. Mix well. Drop by teaspoonfuls onto greased cookie sheet. Bake at 375°F (191°C) for 12 to 15 minutes or until done. Makes 3 dozen cookies.

Sourdough Pumpkin Spice Cookies

Canned yams or sweet potatoes are delicious pumpkin substitutes.

1/4 cup shortening
1/2 cup sugar
1 egg, beaten
1/2 cup sourdough starter
1/2 cup canned pumpkin
1 cup all-purpose flour
2 teaspoons baking powder

1/2 teaspoon salt
1-1/2 teaspoons cinnamon
1/4 teaspoon nutmeg
1/8 teaspoon ginger
1/2 cup raisins
1/2 cup chopped nuts

Cream together shortening and sugar until light and fluffy. Add egg, sourdough starter and pumpkin. Mix well. Combine flour with remaining dry ingredients. Mix well. Add raisins and nuts along with dry ingredients to starter mixture. Mix until blended. Drop by teaspoonfuls onto greased cookie sheet. Bake at 350°F (177°C) for 15 minutes or until done. Makes 1-1/2 dozen cookies.

Sourdough Drop Cookies

The most popular sourdough cookie.

1/2 cup sourdough starter
1 cup evaporated milk
2 cups all-purpose flour
1 cup butter or margarine
1-1/4 cups dark-brown sugar, firmly packed
1 egg, beaten

1/2 teaspoon salt
1/2 teaspoon baking soda
3 cups crushed cornflakes
3/4 cup chopped walnuts
3/4 cup shredded coconut

Stir sourdough starter, milk and 1-1/2 cups flour together in a large bowl. Set aside for 2 hours. In a separate bowl, cream butter with sugar and blend in egg and a mixture of 1/2 cup flour, salt and soda. Stir in cornflakes, walnuts and coconut. Blend both mixtures together. Drop by teaspoonfuls onto a greased cookie sheet. Place mounds about 2 inches apart. Bake at 375°F (191°C) for 15 minutes. Makes 5 dozen cookies.

Sourdough Applesauce Drops

Apple butter may be used instead of applesauce.

1/2 cup sourdough starter
1/2 cup shortening
1 cup sugar
1 egg
2-1/2 cups all-purpose flour
1/4 teaspoon cloves

1/2 teaspoon baking soda
1/2 teaspoon cinnamon
1 cup applesauce, unsweetened
1 cup finely chopped dates
1 cup chopped nuts

Measure out sourdough starter into a large mixing bowl. In separate bowl, cream shortening and beat in sugar. Add egg; beat until light and fluffy. Add to sourdough starter. Mix together dry ingredients. Add dry ingredients alternately with applesauce to sourdough mixture. Drop by teaspoonfuls onto greased baking sheet. Bake at 350°F (177°C) 15 to 18 minutes or until tops spring back under finger tip pressure. Makes 3 dozen cookies.

Sourdough Ambrosia Drops

Helps pretty-up a tray of cookies.

1/2 cup butter or margarine
1/2 cup sugar
1 egg, beaten
1/2 cup sourdough starter
1-1/4 cups all-purpose flour
1/2 teaspoon baking powder

1/2 teaspoon salt
1 tablespoon grated orange peel
1 cup chopped pecans
1 cup coconut
Pecan halves

Cream together butter and sugar until light and fluffy. Add egg and sourdough starter; beat well. Mix together dry ingredients. Add to sourdough mixture along with orange peel, chopped nuts and coconut. Drop by teaspoonfuls onto greased cookie sheet and press a pecan half into the center of each cookie. Bake at 375°F (191°C) for 12 to 14 minutes or until lightly browned Makes 2 to 3 dozen cookies.

Sourdough Sugar Cookies

Egg-yolk paint adds attractive appearance to unbeatable flavor.

Cookies:

1 cup shortening
1-1/2 cups sugar
3 eggs
1/2 cup sourdough starter
1-1/2 teaspoons lemon or almond extract

1 teaspoon vanilla
4-1/2 cups all-purpose flour
1 teaspoon salt
1/2 teaspoon baking soda

Egg-Yolk Paint:

3 or 4 egg yolks
5 teaspoons water

Food Coloring
1 tablespoon white corn syrup

Icing:

3 egg whites at room temperature
1 lb. powdered sugar

1/2 teaspoon cream of tartar

Cookies:

Cream together shortening and sugar. Add eggs, sourdough starter and flavorings. Mix well. Sift together flour, salt and baking soda. Stir flour mixture into starter mixture until well blended. Chill dough, if desired. Roll out dough 1/4-inch thick and cut into desired shapes. Place on ungreased cookie sheet. Bake at 350°F (177°C) until very lightly browned. Remove immediately from oven and from cookie sheet to cool. When cool, paint with egg yolk paint. Use a clean paint brush. If desired, decorate with icing. Makes 4 to 5 dozen cookies.

Egg-Yolk Paint:

Blend together egg yolks, water, desired food coloring and corn syrup to sweeten. If more than one color is desired, divide into small jars before adding the coloring.

Icing:

Combine ingredients. Beat with electric mixer at high speed for 7 to 10 minutes. Icing is now ready to use. Keep bowl covered with damp cloth to prevent drying. Icing becomes very hard when dry.

When cookies are cool, paint with egg-yolk paint, using a clean brush.

Raised outlines are made with icing applied using pastry tube or folded parchment cone.

Sourdough Goo-Goo's

Messy to eat, but oh so good!

Cookies:

1/2 cup sourdough starter
1/2 cup shortening
1 cup sugar
1 egg
1 teaspoon vanilla
1/2 cup cocoa

1/2 cup milk
1/2 teaspoon baking soda
1/2 teaspoon salt
2 cups all-purpose flour
36 marshmallows, cut in half with scissors
1 cup chopped nuts

Frosting:

1 (1-lb). box powdered sugar
1/2 cup cocoa
1/4 teaspoon salt

1 teaspoon vanilla
7 tablespoons boiling water
6 tablespoons soft butter or margarine

Cookies:

Measure out sourdough starter. Cream together shortening, sugar, egg, vanilla and cocoa. Add to sourdough starter along with milk. Mix together baking soda, salt and flour. Add to sourdough mixture and mix until smooth. Drop by teaspoonfuls on an ungreased cookie sheet. Bake at 375°F (191°C) for 8 to 10 minutes. When done, top each cookie with half a marshmallow, cut side down. Return to oven 1 to 2 minutes. Cool and frost with chocolate frosting. Decorate each cookie with a sprinkle of chopped nuts. Makes 36 Goo-Goo's.

Frosting:

Mix powdered sugar, cocoa and salt together. Add vanilla and boiling water. Stir until smooth. Add soft butter and stir until smooth. Frosting thickens as it cools. If it should get too thick, stir in a few drops of hot water.

Sourdough Chocolate Balls

Stored in a pretty container—the perfect gift for the person with a sweet tooth.

1 cup sourdough starter
1-1/2 cups sugar
1/2 cup cooking oil
2 teaspoons vanilla
4 (1-oz.) squares semi-sweet chocolate, melted
3 eggs

1/4 cup powdered milk
2-1/2 cups all-purpose flour
1/4 teaspoon baking soda
1/4 teaspoon salt
1 cup chopped nuts
Powdered sugar

Measure out sourdough starter into large mixing bowl. Add sugar, oil, vanilla, chocolate, eggs and powdered milk. Sift together flour, baking soda and salt. Stir into sourdough mixture. Add nuts; chill. Using about 1 tablespoon dough, shape into balls and roll in powdered sugar. Place on greased cookie sheets. Bake at 375°F (191°C) for 10 to 12 minutes. While still warm, roll again in powdered sugar. Makes 4-1/2 dozen cookies.

Sourdough Chocolate Chip Peanut Mounds

A cookie jar filler-upper!

1 cup sourdough starter
1-1/2 cups brown sugar, firmly packed
1/2 cup shortening
1/2 cup soft butter
2 eggs
2 teaspoons vanilla

1 teaspoon salt
1/2 teaspoon baking soda
3-1/2 cups all-purpose flour
2 cups salted peanuts
1 (6-oz.) pkg. semi-sweet chocolate chips

Measure out sourdough starter. Cream together sugar, shortening and butter. Add eggs and vanilla; combine with sourdough starter. Mix well. Sift together salt, baking soda and flour. Add to sourdough starter. Fold in peanuts and chocolate chips. Drop the dough by rounded teaspoonfuls about 2 inches apart onto a lightly greased baking sheet. Flatten dough with the bottom of a glass that has been greased and dipped in sugar. Bake at 375°F (191°C) for 8 to 10 minutes or until golden brown. Remove cookies immediately from baking sheet. Makes 3-1/2 dozen cookies.

Sourdough Choco-Orange Chippers

You'll love these.

1/2 cup butter or margarine
1 (3-oz.) pkg. softened cream cheese
1/4 cup brown sugar, firmly packed
1/4 cup granulated sugar
1 egg
1/2 cup sourdough starter
1 teaspoon grated orange peel

1/2 teaspoon vanilla
2-1/4 cups all-purpose flour
1/2 teaspoon baking soda
1/2 teaspoon salt
1 (6-oz.) pkg. chocolate chips
1/2 cup chopped pecans
1/2 cup coconut (optional)

Cream together butter or margarine, cheese and sugars. Add egg, sourdough starter, orange peel and vanilla. Blend well. Stir together flour, baking soda and salt. Add to creamed mixture. Add chocolate chips and nuts. If desired, add coconut. Drop by teaspoonfuls onto ungreased cookie sheet. Bake at 375°F (191°C) for 12 to 15 minutes or until golden brown. Makes 3 dozen cookies.

Sourdough Peanut Blossoms

Chocolate kisses make tasty centers for these blossoms.

1/2 cup peanut butter
1/2 cup granulated sugar
1/2 cup butter
1/2 cup brown sugar, firmly packed
1 egg
1 teaspoon vanilla

1/2 cup sourdough starter
1/2 teaspoon salt
1/2 teaspoon baking soda
1/2 teaspoon baking powder
1-3/4 cups all-purpose flour
3 dozen chocolate kisses

Cream together peanut butter, granulated sugar, butter and brown sugar. Add egg, vanilla and sourdough starter. Mix together salt, baking soda, baking powder and flour. Combine with sourdough mixture. Shape into balls and roll in white sugar. Bake at 375°F (191°C) for 8 minutes. Remove from oven and press candy kisses into center of each cookie. Return to oven and bake 2 to 5 minutes. Makes 3 dozen cookies.

Sourdough Jelly Gems

Your favorite jam makes a jewel of a cookie.

1/2 cup butter or margarine
1/4 cup brown sugar, firmly packed
1 egg, separated
1/2 cup sourdough starter

2/3 cup all-purpose flour
1/2 cup finely chopped nuts
1 small jar jam or jelly

Cream butter and sugar together until fluffy. Add well beaten egg yolk; stir in sourdough starter and flour. Chill dough. Pinch off small pieces and roll into small balls—about 1-1/2-inch diameter—dip into slightly beaten egg whites and then into finely chopped nuts. Place on cookie sheet. Make impression in center of each ball. Bake at 350°F (177°C) for 15 minutes. Cool on wire rack. When cool, drop a small amount of jam or jelly in center of each cookie. Makes 2 dozen cookies.

Sourdough Chocolate Brownies

Brownies are delicious frosted with your favorite icing.

4 (1-oz.) squares sweet cooking chocolate
1/2 cup hot water
1 teaspoon baking soda
1 cup butter or margarine
2 cups sugar
4 eggs

2 teaspoons vanilla
1 cup chopped nuts
1-1/2 cups all-purpose flour
1 teaspoon salt
1-1/2 cups sourdough starter

Prepare chocolate mixture by placing cooking chocolate in a small pan and adding hot water; bring to a boil. Stir continuously. Add baking soda and mix. Mixture will foam. Allow to cool to luke-warm. Meanwhile, cream together butter and sugar until fluffy. Add eggs one at a time and beat well after each addition. Add vanilla and the cooled chocolate mixture. Add nuts. Add flour, salt and sourdough starter. Beat well after each addition. Pour batter into a greased and floured 11" x 16" baking pan. Let brownies set in a warm place for 30 minutes. Bake in a preheated 350°F (177°C) oven for 35 to 40 minutes. Makes 16 brownies.

Sourdough Blonde Brownies

Sprinkle chocolate chips over top of warm brownies. Allow to melt and spread to create an icing.

1/2 cup sourdough starter
1/4 cup butter, melted
1 cup light-brown sugar, firmly packed
1 egg
1 cup all-purpose flour

1/2 teaspoon baking soda
1/2 teaspoon salt
1/2 teaspoon vanilla
1/2 cup coarsely chopped walnuts

Measure out sourdough starter. Cream together butter and sugar. Add egg; mix with sourdough starter. Mix together flour, baking soda and salt. Add to sourdough mixture along with vanilla and nuts. Spread in a well greased 8-inch square pan. Bake at 350°F (177°C) about 20 to 25 minutes. Do not overbake. Cut into squares while still warm. Makes 16 brownies.

Sourdough Peanut Butter Brownies

Chocolate and peanut butter combine to make the perfect topping.

Brownies:

1/4 cup shortening
2 (1-oz.) squares unsweetened chocolate
1 cup sugar
1/4 cup peanut butter
2 eggs
1/2 cup sourdough starter

1 teaspoon vanilla
1/2 cup all-purpose flour
1/2 teaspoon baking powder
1/4 teaspoon baking soda
1/4 teaspoon salt

Topping:

1 cup prepared chocolate frosting, page 120
3 tablespoons peanut butter

1/2 cup chopped nuts

Brownies:

Melt shortening with chocolate over low heat. Blend in sugar and peanut butter. Add eggs, sourdough starter and vanilla. Combine flour, baking powder, baking soda and salt. Stir into batter. Spread in greased 9" x 9" x 2" baking pan. Bake at 350°F (177°C) for 20 to 25 minutes. Cool. Makes 1 dozen brownies.

Topping:

Mix frosting and peanut butter. Spread over brownies. Top with chopped nuts and cut into squares.

Sourdough Potato Brownies

Everybody's favorite—made better!

2/3 cup instant mashed potatoes
2/3 cup hot water
1/3 cup shortening
2 (1-oz.) squares unsweetened chocolate
1 cup sugar
2 eggs

1/2 cup sourdough starter
1/2 cup all-purpose flour
1/2 teaspoon salt
1/2 teaspoon baking powder
1/2 cup chopped walnuts

Measure instant potatoes into large mixing bowl. Add hot water and set aside. Melt shortening and chocolate over low heat, stirring constantly. Add chocolate mixture, sugar, eggs and sourdough starter to potato mixture. Stir together flour, salt, baking powder and chopped walnuts. Add to chocolate mixture. Pour into a greased 8" x 8" x 2" square pan. Bake at 350°F (177°C) for 25 to 30 minutes or until done. Cool. Makes 2 dozen brownies.

Topping:

Frost, if desired, by sprinkling semi-sweet chocolate chips over brownies after removing from oven. Allow to set for a few minutes, smooth chips over the top of brownies with a spatula.

Sourdough Applesauce Brownies

Apples and spice and everything nice.

Brownies:

1/2 cup shortening

1-1/4 cups granulated sugar

2 eggs, beaten

1/2 cup sourdough starter

2/3 cup applesauce

1 teaspoon vanilla

1/4 cup milk

1 cup all-purpose flour

1 teaspoon baking powder

1/2 teaspoon salt

1 teaspoon ground cinnamon

1/4 teaspoon ground nutmeg

1/2 cup chopped nuts

Topping:

3/4 cup sifted powdered sugar

1/8 teaspoon ground cinnamon

1/4 cup applesauce

Milk

Brownies:

Cream together shortening and sugar. Beat in eggs, sourdough starter, applesauce, vanilla and milk. Mix together dry ingredients and stir into creamed mixture. Mix in chopped nuts. Spread in greased 13" x 9" x 2" baking pan. Bake at 350°F (177°C) for 25 minutes or until done. Cool before slicing. Makes 2 dozen brownies.

Topping:

Combine powdered sugar, cinnamon, applesauce and enough milk to form a drizzling consistency. Drizzle over slightly warm brownies. Cool.

Cakes

Experienced sourdough cooks know that sourdough is adaptable to a wide variety of cakes and cupcakes. In fact, this method of leavening was used in cake baking long before baking powder was discovered.

When you serve these treats to friends and family, they'll be intrigued with the unique taste that sourdough gives. Lunchboxes will be opened eagerly when they bring Sourdough Malted Cupcakes—not found at any soda fountain! Gingerbread will warm up many a cold evening, Sourdough Pumpkin Roll will replace that standard pumpkin pie for Thanksgiving and your Sourdough Fruit Cake will be worthy of first prize at the county fair!

The flavor of spices, chocolate, fruits and nuts is even richer when used in a sourdough batter. Besides the recipes given here, try adding a half-cup of sourdough starter to any of your favorite cake and cupcake recipes that use baking powder or baking soda. The sourdough will add its unique flavor to your recipes and you will enjoy a different cooking experience.

Sourdough Chocolate Cake

Everyone's favorite enhanced with sourdough flavor.

Cake:

1/2 cup sourdough starter
1 cup water
1-1/2 cups all-purpose flour
1/4 cup non-fat powdered milk
1 cup sugar
1/2 cup shortening
1/2 teaspoon salt

1 teaspoon vanilla
1 teaspoon cinnamon
1-1/2 teaspoons baking soda
2 eggs
3 (1-oz.) squares semi-sweet
   chocolate, melted

Frosting:

3 (1-oz.) squares unsweetened chocolate
1/4 cup butter or margarine
1/2 cup light cream
2/3 cup brown sugar, firmly packed

1/4 teaspoon salt
1 teaspoon vanilla
3 cups powdered sugar (approximate)

Cake:

Combine sourdough starter, water, flour and powdered milk. Let mixture ferment 2 to 3 hours in a warm place until bubbly and there is a clean sour-milk odor. Cream sugar, shortening, salt, vanilla, cinnamon and baking soda. Add eggs one at a time, beating well after each addition. Combine creamed mixture and melted chocolate with sourdough mixture. Stir 300 strokes or mix with electric mixer on low speed until blended. Pour into 2 well greased and floured layer-cake pans or one large 9" x 12" x 2" pan. Bake at 350°F (177°C) for 25 to 30 minutes. Frost with Butterscotch Chocolate Frosting or other icing of your choice. Makes 8 to 10 servings.

Butterscotch-Chocolate Frosting:

In a saucepan combine chocolate squares, butter or margarine, cream, brown sugar and salt. Bring to a boil, stirring constantly. Cook until chocolate is melted. Remove from heat, add vanilla and about 3 cups of powdered sugar for good spreading consistency. Spread over sides and top of cake.

Sourdough Applesauce Cake

A prize winner!

1-1/2 cups sugar
1/2 cup shortening
2 eggs
1 cup sourdough starter
1-1/2 cups applesauce
1-3/4 cups all-purpose flour
3/4 teaspoon cinnamon
1/2 teaspoon ground cloves

1/2 teaspoon ground allspice
1-1/2 teaspoons salt
1/2 teaspoon baking soda
1 teaspoon baking powder
3/4 teaspoon imitation rum extract
1/2 teaspoon imitation butter flavoring
1 cup raisins
1 cup chopped nuts

Cream together sugar and shortening. Add eggs and mix well. Add sourdough starter and apple-sauce. Beat with electric mixer on high speed for 2 minutes. Sift together flour, spices, salt, baking soda and baking powder. Add alternately to starter mixture with rum extract and butter flavoring. Beat after each addition until smooth. Stir in raisins and nuts. Blend well. Pour batter into a well greased and floured tube pan. Bake at 350°F (177°C) for 1 hour 15 minutes or until done. Makes 1 cake.

Sourdough Choco Chip Date Cake

A surprisingly great combination.

1 cup chopped dates
1 teaspoon baking soda
1 cup boiling water
1 cup sugar
1 cup shortening or butter
1 cup sourdough starter

1-1/2 cups all-purpose flour
2 tablespoons cocoa
1 teaspoon vanilla
2 eggs, slightly beaten
1 cup chocolate semi-sweet chips
1/2 cup chopped pecans

Mix together dates, baking soda and boiling water. Cream sugar and shortening. Combine dates and creamed mixture and add sourdough starter, flour, cocoa, vanilla and eggs. Mix well. Add chocolate chips and pecans. Pour into a greased 9" x 12" x 2" pan. Bake at 350°F (177°C) for 40 to 45 minutes or until done. Serve plain, sprinkle with powdered sugar or top with whipped cream and a cherry. Makes 6 servings.

Sourdough Fruitcake

They won't believe it when you tell them it's sourdough.

1-1/2 cups granulated sugar
1/2 cup dark-brown sugar, firmly packed
2 cups butter
4 eggs, well beaten
1 teaspoon vanilla flavoring
1 teaspoon nutmeg
1 teaspoon cinnamon
1/2 cup milk
1 teaspoon salt

1 cup sourdough starter
1/2 teaspoon baking soda
3 cups all-purpose flour
2 cups chopped pecans
1-1/2 cups raisins
1 cup candied pineapple
1 cup candied cherries
1/2 cup candied orange peel

Cream together sugars, butter, eggs, vanilla, spices, milk, salt and sourdough starter. Mix together baking soda and 2 cups flour. Coat nuts and fruit in 1 cup flour. Mix dry ingredients with creamed mixture. Grease two 9-inch loaf pans or one Bundt pan. Line with heavy brown paper that has been greased. Pour batter into pans. Bake at 250°F (121°C) for 3 hours or until done. Makes 2 loaves or 1 Bundt cake.

Sourdough Raisin-Carrot Cake

A great way to make a more-nutritious dessert.

1 cup all-purpose flour
1 teaspoon baking powder
1/2 teaspoon salt
1/2 teaspoon baking soda
1/2 teaspoon ground cinnamon
4 eggs, separated

1/2 cup light-brown sugar, firmly packed
1/2 cup cooking oil
1/2 cup sourdough starter
1 cup coarsely grated raw carrots
1/2 cup seedless raisins
2 tablespoons grated lemon peel

Combine flour, baking powder, salt, baking soda and cinnamon. Set aside. Beat egg whites in small mixing bowl until soft peaks form. Set aside. In a large bowl combine sugar, oil, egg yolks and sourdough starter. Mix in carrots, raisins and lemon peel. Blend in dry ingredients. Fold in beaten egg whites. Turn batter into a well greased and lightly floured 2-quart ring mold or Turk's head pan. Bake at 350°F (177°C) for 30 minutes or until done. Cool in pan on wire rack for 10 minutes. Turn out onto rack to finish cooling. Makes 1 cake.

Sourdough Spice Cake

Sugar and spice make this sourdough sooooo nice.

Cake:

1 cup sourdough starter
1 cup milk
1/2 cup shortening
1 cup sugar
1 teaspoon vanilla
1 teaspoon cinnamon
2 teaspoons nutmeg
1/2 teaspoon cloves

1/2 teaspoon baking soda
1 teaspoon baking powder
2 eggs
1/2 teaspoon salt
2 cups all-purpose flour
1 cup chopped nuts (optional)
1/2 cup raisins (optional)

Caramel Icing:

2 cups light-brown sugar, firmly packed
2 tablespoons all-purpose flour
6 tablespoons milk or cream
4 tablespoons butter or margarine

2 teaspoons vanilla or 1/2 teaspoon
   maple flavoring
1/2 cup chopped pecans

Cake:

Measure out sourdough starter. Add 1 cup milk. In a separate bowl cream together shortening, sugar, vanilla, spices, baking soda and baking powder. Add eggs one at a time, beating well after each addition. Combine mixture with sourdough starter. Beat with a rotary beater or electric mixer 2 minutes. Mix salt and flour together and add to batter. Mix well until batter is smooth. Fold in nuts or raisins, if desired. Pour into 2 greased and floured layer-cake pans. Bake at 350°F (177°C) for 30 to 35 minutes. Test for doneness by pressing center of cake lightly. Cake will spring back if done. Also, cake will shrink slightly from sides of pan. Allow cake to cool for 5 minutes and remove from pan. Cool and frost with Caramel Icing. Makes 1 cake.

Caramel Icing:

Mix sugar, flour, milk or cream and butter or margarine. Boil for 2 minutes. Remove from heat, beat until creamy. Add flavorings. Mix well. Spread on cake and sprinkle pecans on top.

Sourdough Butter Rum Cake

Buttermilk and butter ensure a buttery flavor.

Cake:

2 cups sugar
1 cup butter
4 eggs
1-1/2 cups sourdough starter
1/2 cup buttermilk
2 teaspoons imitation rum extract

1 cup water
2-1/2 cups all-purpose flour
1 teaspoon salt
1/2 teaspoon baking soda
1/2 teaspoon baking powder

Sauce:

1 cup sugar
1/4 cup water

1/2 cup butter
1 tablespoon imitation rum extract

Cake:

Cream together sugar and butter. Add eggs one at a time, beating after each addition. Add egg mixture to sourdough starter. Blend well. Add buttermilk, imitation rum and water. Mix together flour, salt, baking soda and baking powder. Add to sourdough mixture, blending well. Pour batter into a well greased and floured tube or Bundt pan. Bake at 325°F (163°C) for 60 minutes. When baked, pour butter-rum sauce over cake before removing from pan. Cool 5 to 10 minutes before removing from pan. Remove, cool and serve. Makes 1 cake.

Butter Rum Sauce:

Combine sugar, water, butter and imitation rum extract. Pour over cake.

Sourdough Fiesta Cake

Don't spill the beans about the surprise ingredient.

Cake:

1 cup sourdough starter
1/4 cup butter, softened
1 cup sugar
1 egg, beaten
1/2 cup milk
2 cups mashed cooked pinto beans
1 teaspoon vanilla
1 cup all-purpose flour
1 teaspoon baking soda

1/2 teaspoon salt
1 teaspoon cinnamon
1/2 teaspoon cloves
1/2 teaspoon allspice
2 cups diced raw apples
1/2 cup chopped nuts
1 cup raisins
Maraschino cherry halves and chopped nuts

Glaze:

1 cup powdered sugar
1/4 teaspoon vanilla

1 tablespoon butter, melted
1-1/2 tablespoons milk

Cake:

Measure out sourdough starter. In a separate bowl, cream together butter, sugar and egg. Add milk, beans and vanilla. Add to sourdough starter. Mix together dry ingredients and add to sourdough mixture. Add apples, nuts and raisins. Pour into a well greased 10-inch tube pan or Bundt pan. Bake at 375°F (191°C) for 45 minutes or until done. Cool in pan for 5 minutes before removing. Glaze and decorate with fruit and chopped nuts.

Glaze:

Blend all ingredients together and beat until smooth.

Sourdough Carrot Cake

A cake that's worth its weight in gold.

Cake:

1-1/2 cups cooking oil
2 cups sugar
1 cup sourdough starter
3 eggs
1 (8-oz.) can crushed pineapple
2 cups grated carrots
1/2 cup chopped nuts

2 teaspoons vanilla
2-1/2 cups all-purpose flour
3 teaspoons cinnamon
1/2 teaspoon salt
1 teaspoon baking soda
1/2 cup coconut

Cream-Cheese Icing:

1 (8-oz.) pkg. cream cheese
1/2 stick margarine
1 (1-lb.) box powdered sugar

1 teaspoon vanilla
1 tablespoon milk
Chopped nuts (optional)

Cake:

Mix together oil and sugar. Add sourdough starter and eggs, one at a time. Fold in pineapple, carrots, nuts and vanilla. Sift together dry ingredients. Add to sourdough mixture. Blend well. Fold in coconut. Bake in a greased 8" x 12" x 2" pan at 350°F (177°C) for 45 minutes or until done. Cool. Ice with Cream-Cheese Icing. Makes 1 cake.

Cream-Cheese Icing:

Beat all ingredients well. Spread on cooled cake. Sprinkle with nuts, if desired.

Sourdough Streusel-Filled Coffee Cake

Delicious served with any beverage—hot or cold.

Cake:

1/2 cup sourdough starter

3/4 cup sugar

1/4 cup shortening

1 egg

1/2 cup milk

1-1/4 cups all-purpose flour

1/2 teaspoon baking powder

1/2 teaspoon salt

Streusel:

1/2 cup brown sugar, firmly packed

2 tablespoons all-purpose flour

2 teaspoons cinnamon

2 tablespoons butter, melted

1/2 cup chopped nuts

Cake:

Measure out sourdough starter. In a separate bowl cream together sugar, shortening and egg. Add to sourdough starter along with milk, flour, baking powder and salt. Mix well. Spread half of the batter in a greased and floured 9-inch square pan. Sprinkle batter with half of streusel mixture. Add remaining batter and sprinkle remaining streusel over the top. Bake at 375°F (191°C) for 25 to 30 minutes or until done. Makes 1 coffee cake.

Streusel:

Mix ingredients well.

Sourdough Pecan Coffee Cake

The pecan topping is also delicious sprinkled over a fresh apple pie before baking.

1/2 cup butter or margarine
1 cup sugar
3 eggs, beaten
1/2 cup sourdough starter
1/4 cup milk
2 cups all-purpose flour

1 teaspoon baking powder
1 teaspoon baking soda
1/2 teaspoon salt
1 cup sour cream
3/4 cup raisins

Pecan Topping:
3/4 cup brown sugar, firmly packed
1 tablespoon all-purpose flour
1-1/2 teaspoons cinnamon

1/4 cup butter or margarine
1 cup chopped pecans

In a large mixing bowl, cream together butter or margarine and sugar. Beat until fluffy and add eggs, sourdough starter and milk. Mix together dry ingredients and add alternately with sour cream to first mixture. Blend after each addition. Fold in raisins and spread mixture in greased 13" x 9" x 2" baking pan. Sprinkle with pecan topping. Bake at 350°F (177°C) for 30 minutes or until done. Cut into squares for serving either hot or cold. Makes 8 servings.

Pecan Topping:
Mix together brown sugar, flour and cinnamon. Cut in butter or margarine until the consistency becomes crumbly. Mix in chopped pecans.

Sourdough Pineapple Coffee Cake

A great way to brighten your morning, noon, or night.

1 egg, beaten
1/4 cup cooking oil
1 cup pineapple juice, reserved from
   crushed pineapple in topping plus
   water or milk to make 1 cup
1/3 cup sugar

1/2 cup sourdough starter
1-2/3 cups all-purpose flour
2 teaspoons baking powder
1/2 teaspoon salt
1/4 teaspoon baking soda

Pineapple Topping:

1/2 cup sugar
1 teaspoon cinnamon
1 tablespoon butter or margarine, melted

1/3 cup crushed pineapple, drained
   reserving liquid for coffee cake

In large mixing bowl combine egg, oil, juice, sugar and sourdough starter. Mix well and stir in flour, baking powder, salt and baking soda. Beat until smooth. Spread in 8-inch greased baking pan. Sprinkle with topping mixture. Bake at 350°F (177°C) for 35 minutes or until done. Remove from oven and cool 5 minutes before serving.

Pineapple Topping:
Mix all ingredients together in a small mixing bowl.

Sourdough Gingerbread

A gingerbread with more than sugar and spice. Sauce adds sunshine on a cold winter's day.

Gingerbread:

1/4 cup butter or margarine
1/2 cup sugar
1 egg, beaten
1/2 cup molasses
1 cup sourdough starter
1 teaspoon cinnamon
1 teaspoon ginger

1/4 teaspoon ground cloves
1/4 teaspoon nutmeg
1/2 teaspoon salt
1/4 teaspoon baking soda
1/2 teaspoon baking powder
1 cup all-purpose flour
1/2 cup milk

Lemon Sauce:

1/2 cup sugar
1 tablespoon cornstarch
1 cup water

1 tablespoon butter
1 tablespoon lemon juice
1-1/2 teaspoons grated lemon peel

Gingerbread:

Cream together butter and sugar. Add egg and mix well. Add molasses, starter, cinnamon, ginger, cloves, nutmeg, salt, baking soda and baking powder. Add flour and milk and beat well. Bake in a greased and floured 9" x 9" x 2" pan at 350°F (177°C) for 45 to 55 minutes or until done. Makes 6 servings.

Lemon Sauce:

Mix sugar with cornstarch. Gradually stir in water. Cook over medium heat, stirring constantly, until mixture becomes thick. Remove from heat. Stir in remaining ingredients. Keep hot until time to serve.

Sourdough Polish Sweet Bread

Age 8 hours before serving.

Bread:

1 cup sourdough starter
3/4 cup lukewarm milk
1/2 teaspoon salt
3/4 cup sugar
1/4 cup margarine or butter, melted
1/2 teaspoon vanilla

2 eggs, beaten
1/4 teaspoon ground cardamom
1/2 teaspoon baking soda
1/2 teaspoon baking powder
2-1/2 cups all-purpose flour
3/4 cup raisins

Topping:

1/4 cup sugar
1/3 cup all-purpose flour

1/2 teaspoon ground nutmeg
2 tablespoons butter or margarine

Bread:

Measure out sourdough starter. Add milk, salt, sugar, melted butter or margarine, vanilla, eggs and cardamom. Mix together baking soda, baking powder and flour. Add alternately with raisins that have been coated in a small portion of flour. Beat until well blended. Cover with a cloth. Let rise in warm place about 1 hour or until doubled in size. Stir down and turn batter into a greased loaf pan. Sprinkle topping over batter. Cover with a cloth. Let rise 30 to 45 minutes in a warm area. Bake at 350°F (177°C) 30 to 40 minutes or until done. Remove from pans and cool on wire racks. Makes 1 loaf.

Topping:

Mix all dry ingredients together. Cut in butter or margarine with a pastry blender or fork for a crumbly texture. Sprinkle on top of bread mixture.

Sourdough Pumpkin Roll

Use mashed canned yams instead of pumpkin for an interesting variation.

2/3 cup eggs (3 large eggs)
1 cup sugar
2/3 cup canned pumpkin
1 teaspoon grated lemon peel
1/2 cup sourdough starter

3/4 cup plus 2 tablespoons all-purpose flour
2 teaspoons pumpkin-pie spice
1 teaspoon baking powder
1/4 teaspoon salt
Powdered sugar

Filling:
2 (3-oz.) pkgs. cream cheese, softened
4 tablespoons butter or margarine
1/2 teaspoon vanilla

1 cup powdered sugar
1/2 cup chopped pecans

Topping:
1/2 cup whipped cream
2 tablespoons sugar

1 teaspoon vanilla

In a large mixing bowl beat eggs for 5 minutes or until thick with electric mixer. Gradually beat in sugar, pumpkin, lemon peel and sourdough starter. In separate bowl combine flour, pumpkin-pie spice, baking powder and salt. Add all at once to pumpkin mixture; blend well. Pour into a well greased and floured 15" x 10" x 7/8" jelly-roll pan. Bake at 375°F (191°C) for 12 to 15 minutes or until done. Sprinkle powdered sugar on cloth. Turn cake onto cloth. Fold hem of cloth over edges of cake, then roll cake gently, rolling cloth in it. Cool on wire rack, seam side down. When cold, unroll gently, spread filling, carefully reroll, removing towel. Makes 6 servings.

Filling:
Cream together softened cream cheese, butter or margarine, vanilla and powdered sugar. Spread on *completely* cooled cake. Sprinkle with chopped nuts. Roll up. Place on serving dish, seam down.

Turn cake onto cloth that has been sprinkled with powdered sugar. Fold hem of cloth over edges of cake and gently roll up.

When cooled, gently unroll and spread cake with filling.

Sprinkle on remaining ingredients and gently roll up again, this time leaving out the towel.

Sourdough Pumpkin Roll

Sourdough Coffee Date-Nut Loaf

Delicious served with whipped butter or a mixture of honey and butter.

2 cups all-purpose flour
3 teaspoons baking powder
1 teaspoon salt
1/2 teaspoon baking soda
2/3 cup sugar
1/2 cup chopped nuts

3/4 cup chopped pitted dates
1 cup strong coffee
1/2 cup sourdough starter
1 egg, well beaten
2 tablespoons melted shortening or cooking oil

Mix together flour, baking powder, salt, baking soda and sugar. Stir in nuts and dates. Combine coffee, sourdough starter, egg and shortening and add all at once to dry ingredients. Mix together. Turn into a greased loaf pan. Bake at 350°F (177°C) for 1 hour. Makes 1 loaf.

Quick Sourdough Cobbler

Quick and easy with your favorite fruit filling.

1/4 cup butter or margarine
1 cup sourdough starter
3/4 cup milk
1 cup all-purpose flour

1 teaspoon baking powder
1/2 teaspoon salt
1 cup sugar
1 (1 lb. 5 oz.) can pie filling

Melt butter or margarine in a deep-dish casserole. Mix together remaining ingredients, except pie filling. Pour batter over melted butter or margarine. Add pie filling. Bake at 350°F (177°C) for 45 minutes or until done. Makes 1 cobbler that will serve 4.

Sourdough Orange Drops

The delicious flavor of cake-like doughnuts without the bother of rolling and cutting dough.

1-2/3 cups all-purpose flour
1/3 cup sugar
1/2 teaspoon salt
2 teaspoons baking powder
1/2 teaspoon nutmeg
1/4 teaspoon cinnamon

1 egg, slightly beaten
1/2 cup milk
1/2 cup sourdough starter
2 teaspoons grated orange peel
2 tablespoons cooking oil
Cooking oil for frying

Honey Glaze with Coconut:
1/2 cup honey
2 tablespoons boiling water

1-1/2 cups powdered sugar
1-1/2 cups shredded coconut

In a large mixing bowl sift together flour, sugar, salt, baking powder, nutmeg and cinnamon. In a separate bowl combine egg, milk, sourdough starter, orange peel and cooking oil. Gradually add to dry mixture, stirring constantly, until well blended. Drop dough from teaspoons which have been dipped in hot fat to prevent dough sticking to spoons. Use a teaspoon to push dough from another teaspoon into hot fat. Fry in cooking oil at 360°F (182°C) until golden brown. Remove from fat and drain. Dip in honey glaze and roll in shredded coconut. Makes 36 drops.

Honey Glaze with Coconut:
Heat honey in saucepan, add water and sugar. Mix thoroughly. Dip orange drops in warm glaze, drain and roll in coconut.

Sourdough Orange Cupcakes

Add an orange touch to a flavorful dessert.

Cupcakes:

1/2 cup butter
3/4 cup sugar
2 eggs, beaten
1/2 cup sourdough starter
1 cup milk
1/2 teaspoon vanilla
2 cups all-purpose flour

1/2 teaspoon baking soda
1/2 teaspoon baking powder
1/4 teaspoon salt
Grated peel of 1 orange
1 cup raisins
1 cup finely chopped pecans

Topping:

Juice of orange
1/2 cup sugar

Cupcakes:

In a large mixing bowl cream together butter and sugar. Add eggs, sourdough starter, milk and vanilla. Mix well. Mix together dry ingredients and add to starter mixture, beating well. Fold in grated orange peel, raisins and pecans. Fill well greased and floured muffin tins 2/3 full. Bake at 350°F (177°C) for 20 to 30 minutes or until done. Remove from muffin tins and dip in topping mixture. Makes 12 to 14 cupcakes.

Topping:

Combine orange juice and sugar. Heat until sugar has dissolved. Dip muffins in mixture.

Sourdough Pumpkin Cupcakes

A Halloween treat to delight Witches and Goblins.

Cupcakes:

1/2 cup shortening
1-1/2 cups sugar
2 eggs, beaten
2-1/2 cups all-purpose flour
2 teaspoons baking powder
1/2 teaspoon baking soda
2 teaspoons cinnamon

1 teaspoon salt
1/2 teaspoon ginger
1/2 teaspoon nutmeg
1 cup canned pumpkin
3/4 cup milk
1/2 cup sourdough starter
3/4 cup chopped nuts

Orange Cream-Cheese Frosting:

3 tablespoons butter or margarine
1 (3-oz.) pkg. cream cheese,
    room temperature

1/4 cup concentrated orange juice, thawed
4-1/2 to 5 cups powdered sugar

Cupcakes:

Cream together shortening and sugar; blend in beaten eggs. In a separate bowl mix together flour, baking powder, baking soda, cinnamon, salt, ginger and nutmeg. Add pumpkin, milk and sourdough starter to creamed mixture. Stir in dry ingredients; mix well. Fold in chopped nuts. Pour batter into greased or paper lined muffin pans. Bake at 350°F (177°C) for 25 minutes. Cool. Ice with Orange Cream-Cheese Frosting. Makes 10 to 12 cupcakes.

Orange Cream-Cheese Frosting:

Cream together butter or margarine, cream cheese and orange juice until light and fluffy. Gradually add sugar, blending well after each addition until the mixture reaches the right spreading consistency.

Sourdough Malted Cupcakes

A malted dessert that's not all wet.

Cupcakes:

1/2 cup butter, softened
1/2 cup sugar
2 eggs, slightly beaten
1/2 cup milk
1/2 cup sourdough starter
1 teaspoon vanilla

1 cup instant chocolate malted-milk powder
1 cup all-purpose flour
1-1/2 teaspoons baking powder
1/2 teaspoon salt
1/2 cup chopped nuts
8 maraschino cherries, cut in half

Icing:

1 cup powdered sugar
2 tablespoons hot water

1/2 teaspoon vanilla
Dash salt

Cupcakes:
Cream together butter and sugar. Add eggs, milk, sourdough starter and vanilla. Mix together 3/4 cup malted powder, reserving 1/4 cup, flour, baking powder and salt. Add to sourdough mixture; stir until well blended. Fill paper baking cups in muffin pan 2/3 full. Sprinkle with remaining 1/4 cup malted powder and chopped nuts. Bake at 375°F (191°C) for 20 to 25 minutes. Cool and drizzle with icing. Top each with a cherry half. Makes 16 cupcakes.

Icing:
Combine powdered sugar, hot water, vanilla and salt. Spread over cupcakes.

Quick Sourdough Chocolate Cupcakes

Chocolate Lovers Beware! These are so easy to make, you'll prepare them often.

1 cup sugar
1 egg
1/2 cup cocoa
1/2 cup butter or margarine, softened
1-1/2 cups all-purpose flour
1 teaspoon vanilla

1/2 cup milk
1/2 cup sourdough starter
1/2 teaspoon baking soda
1/4 teaspoon salt
1/2 teaspoon baking powder

Measure out all ingredients and put together in large mixing bowl. Do not mix until everything is in the bowl. Mix or beat vigorously, pour into greased or paper-lined muffin pans. Bake at 400°F (205°C) for 18 to 20 minutes. Cool and frost with favorite frosting.

Sourdough Mocha Cupcakes

A subtle chocolate flavor.

Cupcakes:

1 cup shortening
1-1/2 cups sugar
3 eggs
1/2 cup sourdough starter
2 oz. unsweetened baking chocolate

3/4 cup milk
2 cups all-purpose flour
1 teaspoon salt
1/2 teaspoon baking soda
1 teaspoon baking powder

Mocha Icing:

2 cups powdered sugar
3 tablespoons cocoa
2 tablespoons butter, softened

2 tablespoons cold coffee
1 teaspoon vanilla
Few drops milk

Cupcakes:

Cream shortening and sugar together until fluffy. Add eggs and sourdough starter. Heat chocolate and milk until chocolate has melted. Cool; add to sourdough starter mixture. Blend in flour, salt, baking soda and baking powder. Blend well until smooth and free from lumps. Fill greased or paper-lined muffin pans 2/3 full. Bake at 350°F (177°C) for 15 to 20 minutes or until done. Cool and ice with Mocha Icing.

Mocha Icing:

Mix together all ingredients, except milk. Blend until creamy. Add few drops of milk only if needed.

Main Dishes

Sourdough cookery is versatile and limitless. Meat, poultry, seafood and cheese may be combined with sourdough for a wide variety of taste-tempting main dishes your whole family will praise. Sourdough Ham Crescent Rolls can be the main attraction at a luncheon. Make and shape ahead of time, cover with a cloth and refrigerate until ready for use. While you tend to last-minute details, simply remove rolls from refrigerator and allow to rise until time to be baked. A creamed vegetable sauce makes a delicious topping or try one of your favorite cheese sauces.

Sourdough Pizza is authentic old-country Italian. After one bite, you'll be convinced.

You won't be penalized for interference when you interrupt hungry TV sports fans with a platter of Baked Hot Dogs in Sourdough Buns. For those occasions when you forgot to thaw something for dinner, canned tuna makes Sourdough Tuna Fritters that are quick and delicious.

Any time you have leftover dough, use your imagination to create your own main dish. After all, every great recipe was invented by somebody!

Chicken & Sourdough Dumplings

One tablespoon chopped fresh parsley adds color & flavor to this delicious main dish.

Dumplings:

2-1/2 cups all-purpose flour
1/2 teaspoon salt
1/2 teaspoon baking soda
1 teaspoon baking powder
3/4 cup milk

1 egg, beaten
1/2 cup sourdough starter
1/4 cup cooking oil or melted shortening
2 qts. boiling water

Chicken:

2 tablespoons all-purpose flour
3 tablespoons shortening, melted
1 (6-oz.) can evaporated milk
1/2 cup milk
1 (10-1/2-oz.) can cream-of-chicken soup

2/3 cup water
1/2 teaspoon salt
1/4 teaspoon pepper
1/4 cup chopped pimiento
1 (2 to 3 lb.) fryer, cooked, boned,
    cut into bite-size pieces

Dumplings:

In large mixing bowl thoroughly stir together flour, salt, baking soda and baking powder. Combine milk, egg, sourdough starter, and cooking oil or melted shortening. Add to dry ingredients all at once, stirring just till moistened. Drop dough from tablespoon into boiling water. Dip spoon in hot liquid before dropping dumpling each time to help batter slide right off. Cover and simmer for 15 minutes. Remove with slotted spoon, drain and place on top of cooked chicken. Cook, uncovered, at 350°F (177°C) for 10 minutes. Serve hot. Makes 4 to 6 servings.

Chicken:

Over medium heat add flour to melted shortening. Stir constantly while adding evaporated milk, milk, cream-of-chicken soup, water, salt, pepper and pimiento. Add chicken, pour into a 3-quart casserole dish and top with dumplings.

Chicken A La King

An old favorite main dish with sourdough's added zing.

1/3 cup butter or margarine
1/2 cup sliced mushrooms
1 tablespoon minced green pepper
1/4 cup all-purpose flour
1-1/2 cups chicken broth
1 cup milk

1/2 teaspoon salt
1/4 teaspoon pepper
2 cups chopped cooked chicken
1 tablespoon minced pimiento
2 tablespoons chopped parsley
1 egg, beaten

Melt butter or margarine in frying pan over medium heat. Add mushrooms and green pepper; sauté. Add flour, stir and cook until mixture is light brown. Add chicken broth, milk and seasonings. Stir while cooking. Add chicken, pimiento and parsley. Cook until heated throughout. Beat egg in bowl. Add a small amount of hot chicken mixture. Mix well; add to remaining chicken. Stir and cook for 3 to 5 minutes or until thickened. Serve hot over Sourdough Corn Bread Pancakes, page 105. Makes 4 to 6 servings.

Glazed Chicken with Sourdough Biscuits

The flavor of orange marmalade with the convenience of a biscuit mix make this a favorite.

2/3 cup all-purpose flour
1 teaspoon salt
1/4 teaspoon pepper
1 (3 to 3-1/2 lb.) fryer, cut up
1/2 cup cooking oil
1 cup orange marmalade

2-1/2 cups biscuit mix
1/4 teaspoon baking soda
2 teaspoons grated orange peel
1/2 cup orange juice
1/2 cup sourdough starter

Combine flour, salt and pepper; coat chicken with flour mixture. Brown in hot cooking oil in heavy skillet. Cover; cook over low heat for 30 minutes or until tender. Place chicken in greased 11-3/4" x 7-1/2" baking dish. Spread 2/3 cup marmalade over chicken. Combine biscuit mix, baking soda and orange peel in a large mixing bowl. Make a well in the center of dry ingredients. Combine orange juice and sourdough starter; add all at once to well in dry ingredients. Stir with a fork to moisten all ingredients. Turn out onto floured surface and knead lightly 4 to 5 times, adding more flour if necessary. Roll out dough and cut into 2-inch rounds. Place around edge of chicken. Make a dent in top of each biscuit; fill with 1/2 teaspoon of marmalade. Bake at 425°F (218°C) for 12 to 15 minutes or until biscuits are golden brown. Makes 6 servings.

Sourdough Meatball Casserole

New way to top a family favorite.

1 lb. ground beef
1/2 cup mild pork sausage
1/2 cup dry bread crumbs
1-1/3 cups evaporated milk
3 tablespoons chopped onion
1 teaspoon chili powder

1/8 teaspoon pepper
Oil for browning
1 can cream-of-mushroom soup
1 can cream-of-celery soup
1/2 cup water

Biscuits:

1-1/2 cups all-purpose flour
1 tablespoon baking powder
1/4 teaspoon baking soda
1/2 teaspoon chili powder
1/4 teaspoon salt

1/3 cup shortening
1 egg
1/2 cup sourdough starter
1/4 cup evaporated milk
1-1/2 cups grated American cheese

Combine ground beef, sausage, bread crumbs, 1/3 cup evaporated milk, onion, chili powder and pepper; shape into 1-1/2-inch balls. Brown in hot oil. Cover; cook for 15 minutes longer over medium to low heat. Place in 2-1/2-quart casserole. Heat soups, remaining milk and water. Pour over meatballs. Top with biscuits. Bake at 400°F (205°C) for 25 to 30 minutes or until biscuits are golden brown. Makes 4 to 6 servings.

Biscuits:

In a large mixing bowl combine dry ingredients. Using a pastry blender or fork, cut in shortening until mixture is crumbly. Combine egg, sourdough starter and milk; add to dry ingredients, stirring until dough clings together. Turn out onto floured surface and knead lightly for 1 minute. Roll out to a 12-inch square. Sprinkle with cheese; roll up like a jelly roll. Cut into 8 slices. Place on top of casserole with cut side up.

Sourdough Ham Crescent Rolls

Glamorous way to dress up leftover ham. A meal in itself.

Dough:

2 pkgs. dry yeast
1/2 cup warm water (110°F, 43°C)
1 cup sourdough starter
1/2 cup warm milk

1/4 cup sugar
1/2 cup cooking oil
2 teaspoons salt
4-1/2 to 5 cups all-purpose flour

Filling:

2 cups chopped cooked ham
2 hard-cooked eggs, chopped

1 small onion, chopped
1/2 cup cream-of-mushroom soup

Cream Sauce:

1 (10-1/2-oz.) can cream-of-mushroom
 soup, minus 1/2 cup
1 (6-oz.) can evaporated milk
1/8 teaspoon thyme
1/8 teaspoon basil

1 (8-oz.) can green peas, undrained
2 hard-cooked eggs, chopped
Hard-cooked egg slices
Pimiento

Dissolve yeast in warm water. Set aside for 5 minutes. In a large mixing bowl combine sourdough starter, warm milk, sugar, cooking oil and salt. Stir in yeast mixture. Gradually add enough flour to make a moderately stiff dough. Cover with a cloth. Set in warm place free from drafts and let rise for 1 to 2 hours or until almost doubled in size. Punch down dough and divide into 4 parts. Shape each into a smooth ball. Roll out on floured surface in the shape of a circle 1/4-inch thick. Cut each in 8 wedges similar to cutting a pie. Spread with ham filling. Roll up and place on baking sheet. Cover. Allow to rise until double. Bake at 375°F (191°C) for 12 to 15 minutes or until golden brown. Top with cream sauce. Garnish with slice of egg and pimiento.

Filling:

Blend together all ingredients in a small mixing bowl. Spread on cut wedges.

Cream Sauce:

Combine all ingredients, mix well and heat. Serve over ham-filled crescent rolls.

Drop ham filling on the dough. You can spread it out before rolling if you prefer.

Starting at large end of wedge, roll up and place on baking sheet.

Sourdough Corn Bread Chili Bake

A new variation of the ever-popular chili.

1 tablespoon cooking oil
1/3 cup chopped onion
1 lb. ground beef
1/2 teaspoon salt
2 teaspoons chili powder

1/2 teaspoon garlic salt
2 teaspoons Worcestershire sauce
1 (8-oz.) can tomato sauce
1 cup chopped canned tomatoes
1 cup cooked pinto or kidney beans

Batter:
3/4 cup cornmeal
1/4 cup all-purpose flour
2 teaspoons baking powder
1/2 teaspoon salt
1/4 teaspoon baking soda

1/2 cup sourdough starter
3/4 cup milk
1 egg
2 tablespoons cooking oil

Heat oil in skillet. Add onions and ground beef; cook until brown. Add salt, chili powder, garlic salt, Worcestershire sauce, tomato sauce, canned tomatoes and beans. Simmer 15 minutes over medium heat. Place in a greased 2-quart baking dish. Cover with corn bread batter, spreading carefully with wet knife. Bake at 425°F (218°C) for 20 to 25 minutes or until bread is brown. Makes 4 to 6 servings.

Batter:
Mix together dry ingredients in a large mixing bowl. Combine sourdough starter with milk, egg and oil. Add to dry ingredients, blending only enough to moisten. Pour evenly over meat mixture as directed.

Sourdough Skillet Meal

Delicious as a main dish served with a vegetable and crisp garden salad or cole slaw.

1 lb. ground beef
1 large onion, chopped
1 tablespoon cooking oil
1 cup yellow cornmeal
1-1/2 teaspoons baking soda
1/2 teaspoon baking powder
1/2 teaspoon salt
1/2 cup sourdough starter
3/4 cup evaporated milk

2 eggs, beaten
1 (16-oz.) can yellow cream-style corn
1/4 cup cooking oil or melted
   shortening
3 tablespoons cooking oil or
   melted shortening
1/4 cup chopped green pepper
1-1/2 cups grated longhorn cheese

Brown ground beef and onion in 1 tablespoon cooking oil. Set aside. In a large mixing bowl, combine cornmeal with baking soda, baking powder and salt. In a separate bowl mix together sourdough starter, milk, eggs, corn and 1/4 cup cooking oil or melted vegetable shortening. Add to dry ingredients and mix until well blended. In a 10-inch iron skillet heat 3 tablespoons cooking oil or vegetable shortening until hot. Pour in half of cornmeal batter and spoon half of meat mixture over top. Sprinkle with half of green pepper and half of grated cheese. Repeat process, using remaining cornmeal batter, meat mixture, green pepper and grated cheese. Bake at 350°F (177°C) for 45 to 55 minutes or until done. Cut into squares; serve hot. Makes 6 servings.

Sourdough Pizza

Sourdough makes "homemade" pizza better.

1-1/2 cups sourdough starter	Tomato sauce
1 cup warm milk	Sprinkle of salt
1-1/2 teaspoons salt	Sprinkle of pepper
2 tablespoons sugar	Sprinkle of oregano
2 tablespoons cooking oil or	Mozzarella, Monterey Jack and/or
melted shortening	Parmesan cheese
2-1/2 to 3-1/2 cups all-purpose flour	Other favorite herbs and toppings
1/4 cup olive oil	

To sourdough starter add milk, salt, sugar and oil. Add flour 1/2 cup at a time. Stir well after each addition. Add enough flour until dough is too stiff to stir with a spoon. Dough should be heavy but elastic. Turn out onto floured surface and knead 5 to 10 minutes. Place dough in a greased bowl. Cover with a cloth. Set in warm place free from drafts and let rise about 2 hours or until doubled in size. Divide dough into 2 equal parts. Stretch or roll out each part to fit into two 10 to 12-inch round pans. Place dough in pans and press or trim edges to fit. Brush with olive oil. Cover with tomato sauce. Sprinkle on salt, pepper and oregano. Top with cheese or cheeses and other favorite pizza herbs and toppings. Bake at 425°F (218°C) for about 25 minutes. Makes 2 pizzas.

Baked Hot Dogs in Sourdough Bun

A special treat to serve while watching football games on TV.

3/4 cup hot water	1/2 cup sourdough starter
3 tablespoons shortening	1 egg, beaten
1/2 cup sugar	5 to 6 cups all-purpose flour
1 tablespoon salt	24 wieners
1 cup warm water (105° to 110°F)	Melted butter
2 pkgs. dry yeast	

Mix together hot water, shortening, sugar and salt. Stir until shortening is melted; cool to lukewarm. Measure warm water into large warm mixing bowl; sprinkle in yeast. Stir until dissolved. Add lukewarm sugar mixture, sourdough starter and egg. Mix until well blended. Stir in enough remaining flour to make a soft dough. Turn out onto floured surface and knead about 10 minutes or until smooth and elastic, adding more flour if necessary. Place in greased bowl, turning once. Cover with a cloth. Set in warm place free from drafts and let rise 1 to 2 hours or until almost doubled in size. Punch down dough to remove air. Turn out onto floured surface. Cut dough into twenty-four 2-inch balls. Using 1 ball for each wiener flatten and wrap each wiener entirely in dough. Let rise again until doubled in size on greased cookie sheet. Bake at 400°F (205°C) for 20 to 25 minutes or until golden brown. Remove from oven, brush with melted butter. Makes 24 servings

Sourdough Tuna Fritters

Yummy cheese sauce covers these fritters.

2 cups biscuit mix
1 teaspoon seasoned salt
1/2 cup sourdough starter
1 egg, beaten
1/2 cup evaporated milk
2 tablespoons lemon juice

1-1/2 cups tuna
2 tablespoons minced onion
2 tablespoons finely chopped green pepper
2 tablespoons chopped parsley
1/2 cup chopped celery
Cooking oil for frying

Cheese Sauce:
1-2/3 cups evaporated milk
1/2 teaspoon salt

2 cups grated American cheese

Blend together biscuit mix and seasoned salt. Combine sourdough starter with egg, milk and lemon juice. Add to biscuit mix; stir together just until moistened. Add remaining ingredients except cooking oil. Mix well. Drop by teaspoonfuls into 375°F (191°C) cooking oil. Fry for 1 to 2 minutes on each side or until golden brown. Drain on paper towels. Top with Cheese Sauce. Makes 5 servings.

Cheese Sauce:
Simmer milk and salt in saucepan over low heat for 2 minutes; add cheese. Stir until thickened and smooth.

Sourdough Salmon Roll

Nourishing and satisfying for hearty appetites.

Filling:

1/2 cup chopped celery	1/2 cup chopped ripe olives
1/2 cup chopped green pepper	2 tablespoons chopped pimiento
1/4 cup minced onion	1 (1 lb.) can salmon
3 tablespoons butter or margarine	1 (10-1/2 oz.) can cream-of-chicken soup

Dough:

1 cup sourdough starter	4 tablespoons shortening
1 teaspoon sugar	1/2 teaspoon salt
1 teaspoon granulated yeast	1 teaspoon baking powder
2 tablespoons lukewarm water	1-1/4 to 1-1/2 cups all-purpose flour

Sauce:

Milk	Reserved cream-of-chicken soup
Reserved salmon liquid	1 tablespoon lemon juice

Filling:

Sauté celery, green pepper and onion in butter or margarine until vegetables are soft. Stir in olives and pimiento. Drain salmon, reserving liquid, flake salmon and add to vegetable mixture. Stir in 1/4 cup of the chicken soup. Set aside remaining soup for the sauce.

Dough:

Measure sourdough starter into a large mixing bowl. Add sugar. Dissolve yeast in lukewarm water. Add to sourdough starter. Cut shortening into mixture of salt, baking powder and flour, until it resembles coarse cornmeal. Add to sourdough starter, stirring well with a fork. Turn dough out on a lightly floured board and knead gently, adding more flour if necessary. Roll dough out into a rectangle about 9" x 12". Spread dough with salmon mixture and roll up lengthwise, like a jelly roll. Transfer roll to a baking sheet, seam side down. Cover with a cloth. Set in a warm place free from drafts and let rise for 1 hour. Bake at 375°F (191°C) for 30 to 35 minutes or until lightly browned. Serve hot with sauce. Makes 6 servings.

Sauce:

Add milk to reserved salmon liquid to measure 1/2 cup liquid. Combine this liquid with remaining chicken soup. Add lemon juice. Heat to serving temperature.

Cream Sauce Vegetable Topping

Pick your favorite vegetable for this dress-up dish.

3 tablespoons butter or margarine
3 tablespoons all-purpose flour
1 cup chicken broth

1/3 cup light cream
1/4 cup Parmesan cheese
1 cup cooked, drained vegetables

In saucepan melt butter; blend in flour. Add broth and cream all at once. Cook and stir till thickened. Add cheese and vegetable. Blend well. Serve hot over prepared Sourdough Onion Pancakes, page 105. Makes approximately 2 cups.

Curried Shrimp Topping

Curry lovers will enjoy this.

1/2 cup chopped celery
1/2 cup chopped onion
1 clove garlic, minced
1/2 teaspoon curry powder
3 tablespoons butter

1 (10-3/4 oz.) can Cheddar-cheese soup
1 (1 lb.) can whole tomatoes
1 tablespoon lemon juice
Few drops liquid hot-pepper sauce
1 lb. shrimp

Saute celery, onion and garlic in butter. Mix in curry powder. Blend in undiluted cheese soup. Add drained can of tomatoes, lemon juice and hot pepper sauce. Simmer for 15 minutes while cooking shrimp. Cook shrimp, drain, add to curried sauce. Mix together. Serve over Sourdough Cornbread Pancakes or Sourdough Onion Pancakes, page 105. Makes 4 servings.

Health Foods

This section offers a nourishing assortment of sourdough baked goods, including cookies, muffins, breads, rolls and even brownies. All taste delicious and are good for you. Breads and cereals are one of the basic foods necessary for health. Today, with the emphasis on good nutrition, natural breads made from whole-grain cereals without additives and preservatives are popular.

In these recipes, honey and molasses are used instead of refined sugar. Safflower oil is recommended as the least saturated of the vegetable oils. Smaller amounts of salt are used—sea salt if you prefer. Carob is recommended over chocolate; nuts are used for protein; dried fruits give energy, vitamins and minerals needed for good health. All the ingredients blend well with sourdough to offer unique flavor and good health.

The healthful aspects of sourdough have been acclaimed by many nutritionists. In the book *Are You Confused?,* Dr. Paavo Airola notes that people who enjoy exceptionally good health and long life use lots of fermented foods in their diet. Bulgarians eat sour milk, sour vegetables and sour bread. Sauerkraut is an important part of the German diet. Black sour bread is Russia's staple—the average Russian eats 2 pounds of it a day.

Miraculous cures from arthritis, scurvy, ulcers, colds, digestive disorders, even cancer, have been attributed to the regular use of fermented foods. People have eaten these foods for centuries without knowing why they have such a curative effect. Now, German cancer researcher, Dr. Johannes Kuhl, sheds some light on this question. He explains the healing property of fermented foods: "Natural lactic acid and fermentive enzymes, which are produced during the fermentation process, have a beneficial effect on metabolism and curative effect on disease."

There is much debate regarding nutrition. As a home economist, I know that this is an ever-changing science with new discoveries made every day. I wish you success in healthful food planning for your family. I hope these recipes will be of benefit.

Wheat Germ Sourdough Bread

Has the fine flavor that comes from natural ingredients.

1 cup sourdough starter
1-1/2 cups lukewarm water
1 tablespoon brown sugar, firmly packed
1 tablespoon dry yeast
3-1/2 to 5-1/2 cups all-purpose flour

1/4 cup soy flour
1/2 cup wheat germ
1 tablespoon sea salt
1/2 teaspoon baking soda

Glaze:
1 teaspoon sea salt dissolved in
    1 cup cold water

Mix together sourdough starter, water, brown sugar and dry yeast. Stir until yeast is dissolved. Add 2 cups all-purpose flour, soy flour and wheat germ. Beat 4 to 5 minutes. Cover with a cloth. Set in warm place free from drafts for 1 to 2 hours to proof or to make a sponge. Batter will be light and bubbly. Combine salt and baking soda with 1 cup flour and stir into sponge. Add additional flour if necessary, until dough forms a ball and comes away from sides of bowl. Be careful not to add too much flour. Additional flour can be worked in during kneading process. Turn out onto floured surface and knead until smooth and firm. Shape into 2 loaves. Place in greased loaf pans and let loaves rise in a warm place free from drafts for 2 hours or until doubled in size. Preheat oven to 425°F (218°C) and place a pan of boiling water in bottom rack of oven. Brush tops of loaves with glaze, then slash with a sharp knife from end to end, about 1/4 to 1/2-inch deep. Turn oven down to 400°F (205°C). Put bread in oven and bake for 45 minutes. For a darker crust, brush with glaze again and return to oven until crust is as dark as desired. Makes 2 loaves.

Sourdough Pumpernickel Bread

Yeast may be omitted if longer rising time is allowed.

1-1/2 cups sourdough starter
2 pkgs. dry yeast
1-1/2 cups warm water (110°F, 43°C)
1-1/2 teaspoons sea salt
1/2 cup molasses

3 tablespoons cooking oil
2-1/2 tablespoons caraway seed
3 cups rye flour
2-1/2 to 3 cups all-purpose flour or
    whole wheat flour

Measure out sourdough starter. Dissolve yeast in warm water. Add to sourdough starter along with salt, molasses, oil and caraway seed. Mix well. Alternately add rye flour and all-purpose whole wheat flour to make a dough that pulls away from the side of the bowl and is easy to handle. Be sure not to add flour all at once. Add as needed. Turn out onto a lightly floured surface and knead about 5 minutes or until smooth and elastic, adding more flour if necessary. Place in a greased bowl, turning once. Cover with a cloth. Set in warm place free from drafts and let rise about 1 hour or until doubled in size. Punch down the dough. Divide the dough in two equal parts, shape and place in greased loaf pans. Brush with cooking oil. Cover with a cloth. Set in a warm place free from draft. Allow dough to rise 1 to 2 hours or until it is 1/2 to 3/4-inch above the rim of the pan. Bake at 350°F (177°C) for 50 to 60 minutes or until done. Makes 2 loaves.

Sourdough Lettuce Loaf

This moist loaf is best if stored several hours before slicing.

1 cup sourdough starter
1 cup finely chopped lettuce
2-1/2 cups whole wheat flour
2 teaspoons baking powder
1/2 teaspoon baking soda
1/2 teaspoon sea salt
1/8 teaspoon mace
1/8 teaspoon ginger

1/8 teaspoon cinnamon
1 cup honey
1/2 cup safflower oil
1 teaspoon grated lemon peel
2 eggs
1/2 cup milk
1/2 cup chopped walnuts

Measure sourdough starter into large mixing bowl. Chop lettuce. Mix together flour, baking powder, baking soda, salt, mace, ginger and cinnamon. Set aside. Add honey, oil, lemon peel, eggs and milk to sourdough starter along with dry ingredients and nuts, beating well after each addition. Stir in chopped lettuce. Turn into a greased and floured loaf pan. Bake at 350°F (177°C) for 50 to 60 minutes or until done. Cool in pan 15 minutes then invert, remove from pan and cool on wire rack. This moist loaf is best if stored several hours before slicing. Makes 1 loaf.

Sourdough Oatmeal Whole Wheat Bread

High in nutrition and good taste.

1 cup sourdough starter
2 pkgs. dry yeast
1/2 cup warm water (110°F, 43°C))
1-1/4 cups boiling water
1 cup quick-cooking rolled oats
2/3 cup light molasses
1/3 cup safflower oil

1 tablespoon sea salt
5 to 6 cups whole wheat flour
2 eggs, beaten
6 tablespoons quick-cooking rolled oats
1 beaten egg white
1 tablespoon water

Measure out sourdough starter. Soften yeast in warm water. Combine boiling water, oats, molasses, oil and salt. Cool to lukewarm. Stir in 2 cups flour. Beat well. Add to sourdough starter along with softened yeast and eggs. Stir in enough of the remaining flour to make a soft dough. Turn out onto a lightly floured surface and knead 5 to 8 minutes or until smooth and elastic. Shape dough into a ball. Place in lightly greased bowl, turning once. Cover with a cloth. Set in warm place free from drafts and let rise 1 to 2 hours or until doubled in size. Punch dough down. Turn out onto lightly floured surface. Divide dough in half. Cover and let rest 10 minutes. Coat two well greased loaf pans with about 3 tablespoons rolled oats for each pan. Shape dough into loaves. Place loaves in pans. Cover and let rise in warm place free from drafts, 1-1/2 hours or until doubled in size. Brush loaves with mixture of egg white and water. Sprinkle tops lightly with rolled oats. Bake at 375°F (191°C) for 40 to 50 minutes or until done. If tops are browning too rapidly, cover with a tent of aluminum foil for the last 15 minutes. Makes 2 loaves.

Sourdough Peasant Bread

So good for you!

1 cup sourdough starter
1-1/4 cups warm water (110°F, 43°C)
2 pkgs. dry yeast
1/4 cup dark molasses
3 tablespoons safflower oil
2 teaspoons sea salt

1/8 teaspoon baking soda
2 cups whole wheat flour
1/3 cup yellow cornmeal
1/2 cup bran cereal
1 tablespoon caraway seed
2 cups rye flour

In a large mixing bowl measure out sourdough starter. Mix together warm water and yeast until yeast is dissolved. Add to sourdough starter along with molasses, oil, salt and baking soda. Gradually add whole wheat flour, cornmeal, bran and caraway seed. Mix well by hand after each addition, scraping sides of bowl constantly. Stir in rye flour and, if needed, additional whole wheat flour to make a moderately stiff dough. Turn out onto lightly floured surface and knead 5 to 8 minutes or until smooth and elastic. Shape into a ball. Place in lightly greased bowl, turning once. Cover with a cloth. Set in warm place free from drafts and let rise 1 to 1-1/2 hours or until doubled in size. Punch down. Turn out onto lightly floured surface. Divide in half. Cover and let rest 10 minutes. Shape into two loaves and place loaves in two greased loaf pans. Cover and let rise in warm place free from drafts 1 to 1-1/2 hours or until doubled in size. Bake at 375°F (191°C) for 40 to 45 minutes or until done. Remove from pans and cool. Makes 2 loaves.

Sourdough Sunflower Seed Bread

Grow your own sunflowers and try this bread.

1 cup sourdough starter
1 cup milk
1/2 cup molasses
2 tablespoons safflower oil

1-1/2 teaspoons sea salt
2/3 cup hulled sunflower seeds
1/2 teaspoon baking soda
3-1/2 to 4 cups whole wheat flour

Measure out sourdough starter in a large mixing bowl. Add milk, molasses, oil, salt and sunflower seeds. Mix well. Mix baking soda with whole wheat flour. Gradually add to sourdough mixture until dough pulls away from side of bowl. Turn out onto a floured surface and knead about 5 minutes or until elastic. Shape in a ball. Place in a lightly greased bowl, turning once. Cover with a cloth. Set in warm place free from drafts and let rise about 2 hours or until doubled in size. Punch dough down and turn out onto a lightly floured surface. Shape into a loaf and place in a greased loaf pan. Cover and let rise about 1-1/2 hours or until doubled. Bake at 375° (191°C) for 45 minutes or until done. If crust browns too quickly, cover with a tent of aluminum foil for the last 15 minutes. Remove from pan and let cool on wire rack. Makes 1 loaf.

Sourdough Onion-Rye Bread

A heavy, chewy bread with tantalizing flavor.

1 cup sourdough starter
1 pkg. dry yeast
1 cup warm milk
2 tablespoons molasses
1-1/2 teaspoons sea salt
1/4 cup safflower oil

2 tablespoons caraway seeds
1/2 onion, finely minced or
   3 tablespoons instant minced onion
1-1/2 cups whole wheat flour
1-1/2 cups rye flour

Measure out sourdough starter. Dissolve yeast in warm milk. Add to sourdough starter along with molasses, salt, oil, caraway seeds, onion and whole wheat flour. Mix well. Gradually add rye flour until dough pulls away from the side of the bowl. Turn out onto a floured surface and knead about 3 to 5 minutes or until smooth and elastic. Shape dough into a ball. Place in a greased bowl, turning once. Cover with a cloth. Set in warm place free from drafts for 1 to 2 hours or until doubled in size. Punch dough down. Shape in a loaf and place in well greased loaf pan. Brush top with safflower oil. Bake at 350°F (177°C) for 45 to 50 minutes or until done. If bread browns too quickly, cover with a tent of aluminum foil. Makes 1 loaf.

Note:
It is characteristic for this bread to be heavy. You can use more of one flour and less of the other, according to individual tastes.

Sourdough Rye Bread

Equally good served warm or cold.

1 pkg. dry yeast
1-1/2 cups warm water (110°F, 43°C)
3 cups rye flour
1 cup sourdough starter
1/4 cup sugar

3 tablespoons butter, softened
2 teaspoons caraway seed
2 teaspoons sea salt
2 to 3 cups all-purpose flour
1/2 teaspoon baking soda

Soften yeast in warm water. Blend in rye flour, sourdough starter, sugar, butter, caraway seed and salt. Beat well. Combine 1 cup of flour and baking soda. Stir into flour-yeast mixture. Add enough remaining flour to make a moderately stiff dough. Turn out onto floured surface and knead 5 to 8 minutes or until smooth, adding more flour if necessary. Place in greased bowl, turning once. Cover with a cloth. Set in warm place free from drafts and let rise about 1-1/2 hours or until doubled in size. Punch down and divide in half. Cover and let rise 10 minutes. Shape in 2 loaves. Place in greased loaf pans. Cover and let rise until almost double. Bake at 375°F (191°C) for 35 to 40 minutes. Remove from pans and cool. Makes 2 loaves.

Sourdough Granola-Prune Bread

Best-Ever Granola makes this prune bread delicious.

1 cup sourdough starter
1/4 cup brown sugar, firmly packed
1/2 cup raw sugar
1 teaspoon sea salt
2-1/4 cups flour
3 teaspoons baking powder

2 eggs, beaten
1 cup milk
1/4 cup safflower oil
1-1/2 cups granola cereal
1 cup chopped dried prunes, raisins or
  chopped apricots

Measure out sourdough starter. Add sugars and blend well. Mix together dry ingredients. Combine eggs, milk and oil. Add alternately with flour mixture to sourdough and sugars. Beat for 1 minute on high speed. Fold in granola and fruit. Turn into a well greased loaf pan. Bake at 350°F (177°C) for 60 minutes or until done. Cool in pan on wire rack for 5 minutes. Remove from pan. Cool, wrap in plastic wrap and store several hours before slicing. Makes 1 loaf.
Note:
Recipe for Best-Ever Granola is on page 109.

Sourdough Granola-Apple Muffins

How could anything so good be so good for you?

1 cup sourdough starter
1/2 cup milk
1 egg
1/4 cup safflower oil
1/2 cup honey

1 cup applesauce
1/2 teaspoon sea salt
1 teaspoon baking powder
1-1/2 cups whole wheat flour
1 cup granola cereal

Measure out sourdough starter in a large bowl. Add milk, egg, oil, honey and applesauce. Mix well. Mix together salt, baking powder and flour. Add to sourdough mixture. Fold in granola. Stir just until moistened. Fill greased or paper-cup-lined muffin pans 2/3 full. Bake at 400°F (205°C) for 15 to 22 minutes or until done. Makes 12 to 14 muffins.

Sourdough Bran Bread

Delicious way to include bran in your diet.

1 cup sourdough starter
4 tablespoons molasses
1 pkg. dry yeast
3/4 cup lukewarm water
3/4 cup powdered milk
1 egg, beaten

3 tablespoons butter
1-1/2 teaspoon sea salt
1-1/2 cups whole bran cereal
2 cups whole wheat flour
1 to 2 cups all-purpose flour

Measure out sourdough starter in a large mixing bowl. Add molasses and blend well. Dissolve yeast in water. Add to sourdough mixture along with powdered milk, egg, butter and salt. Add cereal and whole wheat flour. Mix well by hand. Add enough all-purpose flour until dough cleans the side of the bowl. Turn out onto a lightly floured surface and knead 2 minutes. Place in greased bowl, turning once. Cover with a cloth. Set in warm place for 1 hour. Punch down. Shape into loaf and place in greased loaf pan. Cover with a cloth. Set in warm place free from drafts for 1 hour. Bake at 375°F (191°C) for 30 to 40 minutes or until golden brown. If top of bread browns too quickly, cover with a tent of aluminum foil. Remove from pan immediately. Makes 1 loaf.

Sourdough Bran Muffins

For muffin lovers of all ages.

1/2 cup sourdough starter
1/2 cup honey
1 egg, beaten
1/4 cup safflower oil
1/2 cup milk

1/2 teaspoon salt
1/2 teaspoon baking soda
1 cup whole wheat flour
1/2 cup whole bran cereal
1/2 cup raisins

Measure out sourdough starter in a large bowl. Add honey, egg, oil and milk. Mix well. Mix together dry ingredients and add to sourdough mixture, stirring just until moistened. Fold in bran and raisins. Fill greased muffin pans 3/4 full. Bake at 400°F (205°C) for 18 to 20 minutes or until done. Makes 10 to 12 muffins.

Sourdough Pruffins

Who wants to eat prune muffins? Call them "Pruffins" and your family will love them.

1 cup bran cereal
3/4 cup milk
1 egg, beaten
1/4 cup cooking oil
1/2 cup sourdough starter
1/4 cup honey

1 cup whole wheat flour
1/2 teaspoon sea salt
2 teaspoons baking powder
2 tablespoons melted butter
4 tablespoons brown sugar
12 pitted prunes

Combine cereal and milk. Let stand until most of moisture is absorbed. Add egg, oil, sourdough starter and honey. Beat well. Mix together flour, salt and baking powder. Add to sourdough mixture, stirring only until combined. Place 1/2 teaspoon melted butter into each of 12 greased muffin cups. Add 1 teaspoon brown sugar and 1 pitted prune in each. Fill each cup 2/3 full with batter. Bake at 400° F (205°C) for 20 to 25 minutes or until tops are golden brown. Makes 1 dozen.

Allow cereal and milk to stand until most of the moisture is absorbed, then add remaining ingredients to make batter.

Place melted butter and brown sugar in bottom of each muffin cup. Add a pitted prune.

Fill each muffin cup 2/3 full with batter.

Sourdough Pruffins and Sourdough Onion-Rye Bread

Sourdough Lemon-Bran Cookies

Bran cookies with an added hint of lemon.

1/2 cup safflower oil	2/3 cup rye flour
3/4 cup honey	1/2 teaspoon sea salt
1 egg	1 teaspoon baking powder
1/2 cup sourdough starter	1/2 cup bran flakes cereal
1-1/2 tablespoons grated lemon peel	1/2 cup wheat germ

In large mixing bowl mix together oil, honey, egg, sourdough starter and grated lemon peel. In separate bowl mix together dry ingredients and add to starter mixture. Blend well. Form dough into 1-inch balls. Place on greased cookie sheet about 2 inches apart. With bottom of a glass flatten dough until it is about 1/4-inch thick. Bake at 350°F (177°C) for 12 to 15 minutes or until golden brown. Allow to cool for a few minutes before removing from cookie sheet. Cookies are very crisp. Makes 2 dozen cookies.

Molasses Cookies

A very crisp cookie.

1/2 cup safflower oil	1/2 teaspoon sea salt
1/4 cup raw sugar	1 teaspoon ginger
3/4 cup molasses	1 teaspoon cinnamon
1 egg, slightly beaten	2 tablespoons wheat germ
1/2 cup sourdough starter	2 cups whole rye flour
3 tablespoons non-fat powdered milk	

In large mixing bowl mix together oil, sugar, molasses, egg and sourdough starter. In separate bowl mix together dry ingredients. Gradually add to starter mixture and blend well. Dough will be very thick. Form dough into balls about 1-inch in diameter. Place the balls about 3 inches apart on greased cookie sheet and flatten the balls with bottom of a glass until they are about 1/4-inch thick. Bake at 350°F (177°C) for 10 to 12 minutes. Cool slightly on cookie sheet before removing. Cookies are very crisp. Makes 3 dozen cookies.

Sourdough Oat-Nut Cookies

A delicious nutty flavor.

3/4 cup raw sugar
1/2 cup safflower oil
1 egg
1/2 cup sourdough starter
1 cup raw rolled oats

1/2 teaspoon sea salt
2/3 cup whole rye flour
2 tablespoons wheat germ
1 teaspoon baking powder
1/2 cup chopped nuts

In a large mixing bowl blend together sugar, oil, egg and sourdough starter. In a separate bowl combine dry ingredients and add to starter mixture. Mix well. Drop by teaspoonfuls onto greased cookie sheet. Bake at 350°F (177°C) for 8 to 10 minutes. Allow to cool slightly before removing from cookie sheet. Makes 3 to 4 dozen cookies.

Sourdough Carob Cookies

Cinnamon and molasses make these a favorite.

1/2 cup butter
3/4 cup raw sugar
1 egg
2 tablespoons molasses
1/2 cup sourdough starter
1-1/2 cups whole rye flour

2 tablespoons wheat germ
1 teaspoon baking powder
1/2 teaspoon baking soda
1/4 cup carob powder
1/4 teaspoon cinnamon

Cream together butter and sugar. Add egg, molasses and sourdough starter. Mix well. In a separate bowl mix together flour, wheat germ, baking powder, baking soda, carob powder and cinnamon. Gradually add to starter mixture and mix thoroughly. Drop by teaspoonfuls onto greased cookie sheets. Bake at 350°F (177°C) for 8 to 10 minutes. Makes 3 to 4 dozen cookies.

Sourdough Carob Brownies

An interesting combination of flavors for a healthful dessert.

1/2 cup safflower oil
1/2 cup raw sugar
1/4 cup molasses
1 egg
1/4 cup carob powder
1/2 cup sourdough starter

1 cup whole wheat flour
2 tablespoons wheat germ
1/4 teaspoon sea salt
1-1/2 teaspoons baking powder
1/2 teaspoon baking soda
1/2 cup chopped nuts

In a medium-sized mixing bowl combine oil, sugar, molasses, egg, carob and sourdough starter. Mix together remaining ingredients. Add to starter mixture and stir until well blended. Spread the batter in an 8-inch greased pan. Bake at 300°F (149°C) for 25 minutes or until done. Cool and cut into squares or desired size for serving. Makes 12 to 14 brownies.

CONVERSION TO METRIC MEASURE

WHEN YOU KNOW	SYMBOL	MULTIPLY BY	TO FIND	SYMBOL
teaspoons	tsp	5	milliliters	ml
tablespoons	tbsp	15	milliliters	ml
fluid ounces	fl oz	30	milliliters	ml
cups	c	0.24	liters	l
pints	pt	0.47	liters	l
quarts	qt	0.95	liters	1
ounces	oz	28	grams	g
pounds	lb	0.45	kilograms	kg
Fahrenheit	°F	5/9 (after subtracting 32)	Celsius	C
inches	in	2.54	centimeters	cm
feet	ft	30.5	centimeters	cm

LIQUID MEASURE TO MILLILITERS

1/4 teaspoon	=	1.25 milliliters
1/2 teaspoon	=	2.5 milliliters
3/4 teaspoon	=	3.75 milliliters
1 teaspoon	=	5 milliliters
1-1/4 teaspoons	=	6.25 milliliters
1-1/2 teaspoons	=	7.5 milliliters
1-3/4 teaspoons	=	8.75 milliliters
2 teaspoons	=	10 milliliters
1 tablespoon	=	15 milliliters
2 tablespoons	=	30 milliliters

LIQUID MEASURE TO LITERS

1/4 cup	=	0.06 liters
1/2 cup	=	0.12 liters
3/4 cup	=	0.18 liters
1 cup	=	0.24 liters
1-1/4 cups	=	0.3 liters
1-1/2 cups	=	0.36 liters
2 cups	=	0.48 liters
2-1/2 cups	=	0.6 liters
3 cups	=	0.72 liters
3-1/2 cups	=	0.84 liters
4 cups	=	0.96 liters
4-1/2 cups	=	1.08 liters
5 cups	=	1.2 liters
5-1/2 cups	=	1.32 liters

FAHRENHEIT TO CELSIUS

F	C
200°	93°
225°	107°
250°	121°
275°	135°
300°	149°
325°	163°
350°	177°
375°	191°
400°	205°
425°	218°
450°	232°
475°	246°
500°	260°

Index

Letter codes shown below follow some recipe titles to indicate the food category.

Bi — Biscuits
Br — Bread
Ca — Cake
Co — Cookies
HF — Health Food

MD — Main Dish
Mu — Muffins
QB — Quick Bread
Ro — Rolls
Pa — Pancake

Spice Chart

NAME AND DESCRIPTION	COMPATIBLE WITH:
Allspice Color—brown Flavor—spicy, sweet, mild, pleasant	All cranberry dishes, spice cakes, beef stew, baked ham, mincemeat and pumpkin pie, tapioca & chocolate pudding
Anise Color—brown with tan stripes Flavor—sweet licorice aroma and taste	Coffee cake, rolls, cookies, all fruit pie fillings, sweet pickles, stewed fruits
Basil Color—light green Flavor—mild, sweet	All tomato dishes, green vegetables, stews, shrimp and lobster dishes
Bay Leaves Color—light green Flavor—very mild, sweet	Vegetables, stews, shrimp, lobster, chicken dishes, pot roasts
Caraway Color—dark brown with light brown stripes Flavor—like rye bread	Cheese spreads, breads and rolls, cookies, vegetables, roast pork
Cardamom Color—cream-colored pod, dark brown seeds Flavor—bitter-sweet	Danish pastry, coffee cake, custards, sweet potato and pumpkin dishes
Cayenne Color—burnt orange Flavor—hot	Deviled eggs, fish dishes, cooked green vegetables, cheese souffles, pork chops, veal stew
Celery Seed Color—shades of brownish green Flavor—bitter celery	Meat loaf, fish chowders, cole slaw, stewed tomatoes, rolls, salad dressings
Chili Powder Color—light to dark red Flavor—distinctive, hot	Mexican cookery, chili, beef, pork and veal dishes, Spanish rice
Cinnamon Color—light brown Flavor—sweet and spicy	Coffee cakes, spice cake, cookies, puddings, fruit pies, spiced beverages, sweet potato and pumpkin dishes
Cloves Color—dark brown Flavor—spicy, sweet, pungent	Ham, apple, mince & pumpkin pies, baked beans, hot tea, spice cake, puddings, cream of pea and tomato soups
Cumin Color—gold with a hint of green Flavor—salty sweet	Deviled eggs, chili, rice, fish
Curry Powder Color—Predominantly rich gold Flavor—exotic with heat	Eggs, fish, poultry, creamed vegetables, chowders, tomato soup, salted nuts
Dill Color—greenish brown Flavor—similar to caraway, but milder and sweeter	Pickling, potato salad, soups, vegetables, salad dressing, drawn butter for shellfish
Ginger Color—tan Flavor—spicy	Cookies, spice cake, pumpkin pie, puddings, applesauce, stews, French dressing

NAME AND DESCRIPTION	COMPATIBLE WITH:
Mace Color—burnt orange Flavor—similar to nutmeg, exotic	Fish, stews, pickling, gingerbread, cakes. Welsh rarebit, chocolate dishes, fruit pies
Marjoram Color—green Flavor—delicate	Lamb chops, roast beef, poultry, omelets, stews, stuffings
Mint Color—green Flavor—sweet	Jelly, fruit salad, lamb and veal roast, tea
Mustard Color—light to dark brown Flavor—spicy, sharp	Pickling, Chinese hot sauce, cheese sauce, vegetables, molasses cookies
Nutmeg Color—copper Flavor—exotic, sweet	Doughnuts, eggnog, custards, spice cake, coffee cake, pumpkin pie, sweet potatoes
Oregano Color—green Flavor—strong	Pizza, spaghetti sauce, meat sauces, soups, vegetables
Paprika Color—red Flavor—very mild	Poultry, goulash, vegetables, canapes, chowders
Parsley Color—green Flavor—mild	Soups, salads, meat stews, all vegetables, potatoes
Pepper Color—black or white Flavor—spicy, enduring aftertaste	Almost all foods except those with sweet flavors. Use white pepper when black specks are not desired.
Poppy Seeds Color—blue-gray Flavor—crunchy, nutlike	Breads and rolls, salad dressings, green peas
Rosemary Color—green Flavor—delicate, sweetish	Lamb, beef, pork, poultry, soups, cheese sauces, potatoes
Saffron Color—red-orange Flavor—exotic	Rice, breads, fish stew, chicken soup, cakes
Savory Color—green Flavor—mild, pleasant	Scrambled eggs, poultry stuffing, hamburgers, fish, tossed salad
Sesame Seeds Color—cream Flavor—crunchy, nutlike	Breads and rolls, cookies, salad dressings, fish, asparagus
Tarragon Color—green Flavor—fresh, pleasant	Marinades of meat, poultry, omelets, fish, soups, vegetables
Thyme Color—olive green Flavor—pleasantly penetrating	Tomato dishes, fish chowder, all meats, potatoes
Turmeric Color—orange Flavor—mild, slightly bitter	Pickles, salad dressings, seafood, rice